THE HOW OF
AUDIENCE DEVELOPMENT
FOR THE ARTS

LEARN THE BASICS, CREATE YOUR PLAN

SHOSHANA DANOFF FANIZZA
AUDIENCE DEVELOPMENT SPECIALISTS

ISBN: 978-1-4834-3409-4 (sc)

Lulu Publishing Services rev. date: 07/22/2015

CONTENTS

SPECIAL THANKS

The printed version of this book would not have been possible without the following people.* Thank you for your contributions, your support, and for your faith in my audience development work for the arts.

In order of contribution amount:

Jean Quenon
Richard Quenon
Ron Evans
Thomas Jacquat
Ann Peters
Liz Day
Holly Hickman
Dale Matt
Evan Quenon
Ilana Rudnik
Deborah Wallace
Leah Danoff
Nancy Filice
Harold Gray
Tara Lapointe
Doug Moran
Travis Bedard
Kathryn Denton
Al Stilo
Silagh White
Stephen P. Brown
Alexis Del Palazzo

* Thank you to the anonymous contributors. You know who you are, so thank you!

INTRODUCTION

I received an email from an audience development manager of a symphony in Texas. He was intrigued by my website and services yet mentioned how jaded he was of not getting value for his money in the past when it comes to working with consultants. He wanted to know if I could supply him numbers for proof of my audience development skills to see if I was worth it or not. I corresponded back with my enthusiastic numbers. However, I'm not sure this manager completely knew what audience development is about. If all he cared about were the numbers, then he really didn't know. What mattered to me after this interaction was the fact that this person solidified the case for the need to define audience development. Audience development is a buzz word right now, and it is a necessary component for the arts all around the world. Small and big artists and arts groups need it; small and big budgets need it. However, does anyone really know what audience development is?

Despite the fact that we are growing technology wise by leaps and bounds, and have the ability of creating big numbers, perhaps we have taken a step back when it comes to our people skills. We are forgetting that the "number" is a person with a personality. If all we seek are numbers, our audience could spike temporarily, but this increase will not last long term. Our convenient technology is one of the culprits in creating this pattern.

For example, we have the capability of buying a ticket online and going to a show without speaking to anyone in the organization. Is this a good advancement then? With the new technology, we are losing touch with being in touch. We are attempting to mass market ourselves into a better predicament. Mass marketing is not using a personal touch. What is even more fascinating is the fact that the same technology that is keeping us humanly apart is attempting to put us back together again: social media, discussion boards, online match making, online customer service and chat rooms. Yes, we can use these tools for good, however, the personal, organic contact is still being lost. No wonder we are all struggling with knowing who are audiences are, what would make them happy, and puzzling about how to reach them since we have forgotten how to be personal.

The other main culprits to this breakdown of personal communication I attribute to our "capacity issues." Staff, time and money could be an excuse for our deterioration of people skills along with our unwillingness to attempt something new, something different than the status quo way of attempting to gain and increase our audiences. "We don't have the time or enough staff to dedicate," some say.

In our arts businesses, we used to thank Mr. Tom Audiencegoer, in person, and answer all his questions, in person, and get to know him while he was purchasing his tickets, in person, and later thank him for coming to the show, you guessed it, in person. These days we are lucky if we even know Tom's name, let alone any of his buying habits or his personal demographics (or psychographics) such as who is a part of his family, why he enjoys coming to the shows, what he does in his spare time, what he does for a living, and what his likes and dislikes are, who Tom is as a person. Individual artists have the benefit of selling their art in person at times, but so many of them are taking the mass marketing, easy technology route, and they too are losing their audience or not gaining one in the first place.

This means, the people are still out there, but we simply do not know our patrons personally anymore. To add to this, the amount of people that we do personally know is a shrinking number each year. The one demographic most of us are in touch with, the older demographic, is the demographic that we are naturally losing. We all know our main audiences are naturally shrinking. However, this demographic enjoys buying the old fashion way, the audience development way, and if we don't treat them right, we serve to lose them before their time. We also serve to lose a new generation of audience if we keep clunking along with the same tired methods to gain an audience. We are losing touch with the newer generations before we are able to gain their attention.

Our losing touch can make our patrons lose touch, and everyone in our business knows how expensive that can be. Right now our solution has been to use marketing attempts to reach out using targeted methods. What I have learned is that it takes 9 times for a marketing message to be effective: three times to get their attention, three times to think about it, and three times to get someone to purchase.

Most organizations also tend to spend more of their marketing budgets for single ticket patrons than on their subscriber programs, special events, and other longer term audience development goals. Isn't this awfully backwards? Getting to know your audience and serving them the way that they would like to be served, by putting money into programs that make this happen, will serve artists and arts organizations better in the long run. This will also help everyone to save money. Subscriptions are not working, you may say, but if the audience becomes more involved, they will be sold on subscriptions too. Plus, there are new ways to make subscriptions attractive again by working with your audience so they have more of a choice.

The majority of surveys I have viewed are indicating that the number one reason people attend a performance is due to hearing about it from a friend or family member. You will learn that the power of people, people energy is extremely valuable.

To me it makes sense (and cents) to bring back the personal touch, to bring back building relationships with our patrons. Marketing is a useful tool to get the information out, but we still will be dealing with a faceless audience that will be fickle in their decision to purchase another single ticket. Audience development has a face, a personality, and the ability to form solid relationships and collaborations with the people of our communities. Audience development also will bring happier and more loyal audiences, or rather the perfect match of an audience for our art form, something all of us can use!

In this book, I will explain what audience development is and the components of audience development which will include a full discussion on the 4 C's of audience development. You will learn the "how" of audience development: how to make a plan, how to choose what audience relations program will work for you, how to brand so your audience has a clear understanding up front as to who you really are, and how to find and build on the resources you already have.

I have also included a sneak peek of my next book, *The Tao of Audience Development.*

Since this book was originally created for an eBook version, you will still see the links that I created via underlined words or url addresses. If you are curious as to where the links take you, or to get more information, the eBook version is still available for purchase.

All in all, I felt it was the right time to finally define, ponder and discuss our wonderful buzz word, audience development, and I hope you will become as passionate and as fond of audience development as I have.

Cheers to happy and loyal audiences,
Shoshana Fanizza
Founder of Audience Development Specialists

WHAT IS AUDIENCE DEVELOPMENT?

HELLO, MY NAME IS AUDIENCE DEVELOPMENT.
(IT IS SO NICE TO MEET YOU!)

Right off the bat, I want to combat the definition of audience development as being obtaining "butts (or cheeks or bums) in seats." The audience development I know and love is more dignified with way more depth. Yes, we can all use more "butts in seats," and it is a technique that will make you appear to be successful temporarily, but what we really need is more people in seats that continue to be loyal people in seats. The best way to get more people in seats that will continue to be loyal people in seats is to get to know the people. Audience development is about building relationships with your patrons and getting to know them personally.

In this book audience is being defined as a group of people that connect with your art. You can have many different types of audiences for your art.

Audience development has been a buzz word in the past 3-6 years in the U.S. (England, Scotland and Canada have been using it for many years), yet so many people still view it as "butts in seats." This definition implies that audience development is only for arts organizations that sell tickets. It also implies that it is marketing geared to getting butts in the seats. Again, this definition is not audience development.

Audience development is relationship building at its best. It is utilizing people power, the power of people energy, to increase exposure and awareness of your art form and/or organization. It is building existing and potential audience bases, fan bases, patron support (donors, sponsors and volunteers) by focusing on relationships, which will get the right kind of people more involved with your art form and/or arts organization. Imagine building your own community of support, your own art family. Who are the people that will really dig your art form (existing and potential)? What kinds of people are they? Then after you find your people, you can target which ones have the talent and desire to spread the word, volunteer, donate, become subscribers, be on your board, etc.

I have searched high and low for a good definition and gave up due to the Goldilocks complex: this one is too soft and simplistic - this one is too hard to understand. I decided to create my own definition, and this one felt just right to me.

"Audience Development is the building of relationships with your existing and potential audiences, through the use of specific audience relations programs, in order for them to become more involved with your organization and/or art form. Audience development uses the 4 C's: Community, Connections, Collaborations, and Caring."

Let's pick apart this definition. We are getting the point now that audience development is about building relationships, but with whom?

We want to build relationships with our **existing audience**, the people that are already attending and purchasing. Building relationships with this audience can help us reach out to similar people, which is **broadening** our audience. Building relationships with our existing audience can also serve to get this audience more involved or to **deepen** our audience.

We also want to build relationships with our potential audience, with people that have yet to become involved with our art. This is known as **diversifying** our audiences. You can't diversify your audiences long term unless you build relationships first.

The **audience relations programs** are the programs that you develop to be a part of your audience development plan. These programs will also serve to **deepen** your relationships with all of your audiences in order to deepen their relationship with you and your art.

All audience development plans should incorporate the 4 C's of audience development. We will dive more into the 4 C's a little later, but without having all 4 C's as part of your audience development plan, your plan will not be complete and will not function as well.

BUT, I STILL NEED "BUTTS IN SEATS"

So I sense you are still not convinced about the definition of audience development, and maybe it is good timing for me to continue the subject of "butts in seats." I was recently contacted by an organization that was in need of filling their seats, "we need butts in seats!" They needed someone who could guarantee "butts in seats" in order to make their sponsors happy. I completely understand the bottom line. Funding is necessary to continue their program. However, fulfilling this bottom line in this manner does not guarantee that the bottoms they are filling it with will return again.

Let's finally define "butts in seats" for what it really is. "Butts in seats" is a series of short term marketing pushes to paper the house. "Butts in seats" can bring short term rewards like creating the facade that you are successful in filling the house, but in the long term, you are actually taking the focus away from building an audience that will commit to you and your art form. The percentage of returning butts as a result of these types of consuming initiatives (time and money) is low.

Audience development is a long term initiative (takes time, but less money); it is about building relationships with the right people. This focus will build your audience and fill the seats with people that not only will want to come back time and again, but are likely to become more involved with your art and/or organization by subscribing, volunteering and donating. It may take more time to build, but it is well worth it. In the end, you won't need to work as hard since all of those never ending bursts of costly marketing pushes will become less necessary as you go along.

Furthermore, your art form took years to perfect. Wouldn't it be wise to approach something as important as building the right audience with the same diligence? Being diligent means that you know about and use the 4 C's of audience development.

GET TO KNOW THE 4 C'S

If you don't know about the 4 C's of audience development, it is time to find out about them. You're in luck! Here is a quick course:

1. Connections – Connections open the doors to a variety of possibilities for increasing audience, volunteers, sponsors and donors. Connections are your family, friends, colleagues, neighbors, co-workers, you name it. Anyone that you have some form of relationship with is one of your connections. Your connections are the people that will want to support you and are the people that need to be asked when you need help. They are your people power. I will discuss about planning for people power later on in this book.

2. Collaborations – Collaborating makes big things happen and sharing and expanding your audiences won't hurt you either. There are many ways to collaborate with another entity:

- Programming collaborations – pretty self explanatory, but I challenge you to come up with new mixtures.
- Marketing collaborations – this could mean trading lists, cross promoting using emails or coupons, or sharing ad space to save money.
- Collaborating with a social cause – you can use a special event or concert to donate a portion back to a social cause – be sure to figure out which cause rings true for your audience and which organizations are energetic enough to help provide you with an audience.
- Office space collaboration – with office space getting pricier, join up with another organization to share the costs of a nice space!
- Community box office – more and more smaller arts organizations are going this route, creating one box office

for a group of organizations. One concern though – make sure that each organization is well cared for customer service wise and that audience information for each organization is captured for follow up. Some community box offices don't have time to collect patron information, and this could make a big difference in obtaining or not obtaining repeat patronage.

- Collaborating with corporations – similar to sponsorship, except perhaps you would be providing entertainment or art for their corporation in return for their support – turn your sponsorships into partnerships!

- Community Outreach collaborations – two of my favorites are collaborating with the local libraries and the local farmers' markets – both provide great spaces and opportunities to reach the public, and they help promote and advertise for your special outreach event!

- Business collaborations – cross promotions with businesses that make sense for your audience – make sure this is in compliance with non-profit laws before proceeding.

- Restaurant and Transportation collaborations – find local transportation and restaurants willing to collaborate on giving your patrons a deal off of their meal if they can show their tickets or season subscription card.

- Gala collaborations – yes, I saw this in an article today. Two organizations combined their galas since they knew that they shared an audience. The patrons were happy that they didn't have to go to two separate events and the organizations saved costs while still obtaining funds equal to amounts that they usually receive.

As you can see, collaborating is smart on so many levels. Collaborations will help you build all of your 4 C's while at the same time saving you some C notes!

3. Community – Becoming a part of your community will increase awareness of you and potentially help to increase your audience. You can also look at this C word as building your own community that surrounds and supports your art/organization, and becoming a part of your community will help you to do this since you will be showing others in your area that you care about them.

4. Caring - Showing your connections, co-workers, community and your audience that you care about their wants and needs will endear them to you even more and increase the likelihood of them continuing their relationship with you and getting them more involved.

Let me give you an example of how the 4 C's can work in your favor: The Parlando School for the Arts here in Boulder, CO used all 4 C's during their run of the *Secret Garden,* and reaped the benefits with sold out shows, overflow seating and standing room only. The buzz was fantastic for them! Their directors used their New York Broadway **connections** to acquire some fabulous guest directors to instruct workshops and add guidance during the rehearsals. They built a sense of **community** by inviting actors and singers from 19 different colleges, high schools, and middle schools around the Front range. The musicians came from Boulder County and beyond as well. In order to make this production magical in their sets, their **connections** became **collaborations** among Cirque du Soleil, Dreamworks and the makers of The MATRIX. And finally, you can tell that they **care** about their directors, cast and musicians since I received an invitation personally from one of the musicians. Let me tell you, a musician would not waste their time to send out invites unless they felt cared for. The audience received a special thank you after the event as well.

So if you are interested in selling out shows, increasing your flock of fans, and building a bigger pool of volunteers, sponsors and donors, put all 4 C's into your action plan, and you will reap the benefits too.

IS THERE A 5TH C?

Like the debate of the 5th Beatle of the Beatles*, my favorite band, people have been wondering if there is a 5th C and what C would be considered the 5th C. One night, I did an hour consultation meeting with the Colorado Wind Ensemble. I quickly explained about the 4 C's of audience development. While speaking to them, I naturally found out that there were two other C's that could take the title: **Courage and Commitment**.

Audience development takes **courage** for many reasons. For one, you need the courage to be able to take the steps to build relationships with people. Building relationships takes a bit of moxy. You need the courage to ask someone to have a cup of coffee with you. It takes courage to mingle and to ask people questions to get to know them better.

Secondly, it takes courage to ask your connections to help you. Many people have trouble asking their friends and family for help and figure they don't want to bother them. They spend their time attempting to network with people they barely know and ask these new people for help. That's what networking is about, right? However, think about who cares about you and who wants you to succeed in life – your friends and family! Not asking your friends and family to volunteer, donate, connect you with a good connection is like cutting yourself off from your main life support. Do get over your personal discomforts and get up the courage to ask your friends and family for help. You will find a better network of real relationships naturally building for you to help build support for your art.

Lastly, it takes courage to try something new and different than what we have been doing all along. This is a new way of building your

---

* Inconsequentially, I happen to regard George Martin as the 5th Beatle. George Martin helped the Beatles to find their revolutionary sound time and time again!

audience; it is different than the typical marketing and networking that we have learned to work with over the past few decades. Build up the courage to take the risk and try audience development. Move some of your marketing budget to an audience development line and start creating audience relations programs. I can guarantee you that the time and efforts and the small amounts of money you give to audience development will build your audiences, your volunteer base, and your donor support. One of the popular reasons people go to art functions is through a suggestion from a friend or family member. I am seeing that these numbers on surveys are starting to surpass marketing and publicity put together. Audience development, the personal, one-on-one approach to spreading the word works!

It will also take **commitment** to create a plan and follow through, making changes as necessary, but never faltering or swaying from this new mentality. Audience development may cost less, but it does take more time and effort. You will need to be committed to the process. The good news is that if you commit and develop a team of people to support you, you will see results.

With courage and commitment, there is nothing to fear. Use these 5th C's of audience development to take you to the next level. Take the risks to build a better audience using good old fashioned courage and commitment, and you will see a world of support unfold for you.

WHO NEEDS AUDIENCE DEVELOPMENT?

Every artist and arts organization needs audience development since every artist and arts organization needs people power or people energy. Every type of artist and arts organization needs support.

For one, audience development goes way beyond "butts in seats", as we have already established. It is instead about building relationships with people that in time will become fans of the art that you are presenting. People that become fans are more likely to invest their time in helping your art to succeed, either through steady patron support, donating money, sponsoring or volunteering their time.

Of course this does translate into selling more tickets and it is easy to see why audience development is important to performing arts organizations in this sense, but it also translates into financial success for the individual artist. Can you imagine how beneficial a fan base can be for an individual artist? I have an example for you.

Last year, I was hired by a local musician (Rosh) since he wanted to build his audience. At that time, he was able to book gigs in smaller venues like coffee houses, but he desired to go beyond these venues to get bigger gigs and be booked by bigger venues. In order for these bigger venues to book him, he had to prove that he has a consistent fan base that will fill their bigger houses. After learning and using audience development techniques, he was able to go from 20 people to around 120 people (in two gigs), thus getting closer to being booked by bigger venues! Currently, he is a producer of a well received concept called The Blind Cafe™, and he is being booked (they contact him now) all over the country with sold out shows.

In terms of a visual artist wanting to be booked by a gallery, wouldn't a gallery book an artist faster knowing that the artist had a big following? The gallery wants to ensure big crowds as well. The more popular an artist is, the easier the artist will be booked for their own show. Not to mention the fact that selling their art or finding funding or commissions for creating their art will become easier.

So, is audience development only for performing arts organizations that sell tickets? As you can see, I have pointed out that all artists can benefit from audience development. Going beyond "butts in seats" and viewing audience development as developing relationships with people can make a huge difference for every type of artist. Audience development can benefit all artists in a positive way by helping them to gain a bigger fan base for their art, which will move them towards a brighter financial future and an expanded artistic life.

Wouldn't it be wonderful to sustain yourself by creating and sharing the art that you love? Audience Development can help make it a reality!

THE CASE FOR AUDIENCE DEVELOPMENT

AUDIENCE DEVELOPMENT AND MARKETING

Right now many people view audience development as an additional expense. "If I already have marketing, why do I need audience development?" or "We need to cut back, I simply can't add audience development right now." or "Maybe I should apply for a grant for audience development to receive funding, but we are not sure what extra we can do." or "We are not sure we have the time to do this grant with everything else on our plates."

I'm using this moment to put out into the universe that audience development can support the arts, but only if a shift in our everyday thinking occurs. For decades we have relied on marketing and PR to get an audience. We have also been using marketing to build donor and volunteer support. Is marketing alone working? Is spending all that money on advertising getting the needed results? If it were, I don't think the arts would be in the predicament it is now. Do you feel like you are banging your head against the wall trying to get results from doing the same old thing? Well, maybe some of us feel this way.

Albert Einstein once wisely said, "Insanity: doing the same thing over and over again and expecting different results."

Maybe a change is needed so we stop the insanity. I feel that audience development is the change we need.

When looking at organizations that are doing okay despite the economy, I have been finding that these organizations are naturally using audience development, whether they realize it or not. They are using the 4 C's. Again, if you do not have elements of connection, community, collaboration and caring, you are going to fall short on gaining the right audience for your art and/or organization. If you don't have a solid plan with the right audience relations programs, you may not reach your goals.

I feel that people are confused about whether or not audience development is something different than marketing.

Let's define what marketing is:

From Wikipedia[1]:

Marketing is a business term referring to the promotion of products, advertising, pricing, distribution channels, and branding. The American Marketing Association (AMA) states, "Marketing is an organizational function and a set of processes for creating, communicating and delivering value to customers and for managing customer relationships in ways that benefit the organization and its stakeholders."

Professor E. Jerome McCarthy, ... at the Harvard Business School in the early 1960s, suggested that the Marketing Mix contained 4 elements: product, price, place and promotion.

and Audience Development (my definition):

Audience Development is the building of relationships with your existing and potential audiences, through the use of specific audience relations programs, in order for them to become more involved with your organization and/or art form. Audience development uses the 4 C's: Community, Connections, Collaborations, and Caring.

In view of these two definitions, it seems to me that marketing is creating and promoting a product that you think your audience is going to want or rather creating for your audience to benefit the organization. Audience Development, on the other hand, is working with and creating *with* the audience to benefit both the organization and the audience.

Marketing is about getting the information out. Audience Development also gets the information out, but uses word of mouth and other personal approaches instead of the more costly mass advertising that may or may not work. As I mentioned, I like to call these programs and ideas audience relations programs. The personal approach usually does work. For example many people would agree that word of mouth is still the best advertisement of them all. Word of mouth is about relationships, thus it is a part of audience development.

Now a good marketer uses audience development, meaning that they attempt to build relationships with their customers. However, audience development, although you can tweak marketing techniques to be more personal, does not have to use typical marketing to be effective.

When I was a marketing director, it wasn't until I added in audience development components that I saw a major difference in my audience. To be honest, it was the audience development that helped me to sell out a show, not the marketing, and the proof was in the surveys and feedback.

WHAT ABOUT RELATIONSHIP MARKETING?

In the past, I have participated in interesting discussions about whether or not the term "audience development" was simply a new term for something old, "relationship marketing."

Wikipedia[2] defines relationship marketing as:

Relationship marketing is a form of marketing developed from direct response marketing campaigns conducted in the 1970s and 1980s which emphasizes customer retention and satisfaction, rather than a dominant focus on point-of-sale transactions.

Relationship marketing differs from other forms of marketing in that it recognizes the long term value to the firm of keeping customers, as opposed to direct or "Intrusion" marketing, which focuses upon acquisition of new clients by targeting majority demographics based upon prospective client lists.

Relationship marketing involves the application of the marketing philosophy to all parts of the organization.

I have to admit that from the above definition, audience development certainly uses relationship marketing. However, and a big however at that, audience development is, in my opinion, so much more. Audience development has a specific task attached to it – developing an audience. Yes, it uses the building of relationships to do this, but the specific task of evolving the audience member from a one-time interest buyer to a happy, loyal and involved patron is what sets audience development apart from the generic relationship marketing.

The fact that the definition of relationship marketing goes on to suggest that the main benefit is "to develop one-to-one marketing offers and product benefits," separates audience development from relationship marketing further. Audience development is not used simply to be able to market one-on-one, but to actually get to know the patrons in order to build a sense of partnership, to get the patron involved (not just a customer of your "products"). Also, audience development is not just about the artist or organization relating to the patron one-on-one, but serves to establish relationships between patron and patron. Audience development builds a sense of community among all the patrons, something that relationship marketing does not do.

Lastly, relationship marketing seems to be a means to obtain a customer and to keep a customer, while with audience development this goal is still the after thought, what naturally happens. The goal of true audience development is the relationship. Treating the customer as a friend is relationship marketing. Making friends for life is audience development.

All in all, audience development uses the "relationship" part of relationship marketing, but doesn't necessarily use the "marketing" part. To me, audience development is a unique entity all its own and something well worth pursuing.

IS IT EXPENSIVE?

In these uncertain economic times we also need to consider the costs of marketing vs. audience development. Marketing can be pricey. An average ad can cost $500 (or more, but for the sake of an easy example, $500). As I mentioned before, it usually takes 9 times (9 ads) for a person to purchase (3 times to get their attention, 3 times to get them to consider, and 3 times to actually purchase). This adds up to $4,500 per campaign. Some marketers use even more money per campaign.

Let's take a second to review the costs of audience development. Audience development, on the other hand, starts at free or as little as the price of a cup of coffee. It may cost a little bit for hiring someone to guide you and help you with planning. It may also cost you a little bit of salary time to design the plan and implement, but the overall costs are less than marketing, which still needs this planning and coordination time.

Now, if marketing is not working as well as it used to (mainly due to people getting inundated with so many marketing pitches every day), why not try something different? Why not try shifting some of your marketing budget into an audience development line? You will not have to spend extra money. Instead you will be using your budget more wisely, placing money on a plan and programs that actually will work for a fraction of the cost of typical marketing.

I have seen many artists and organizations decide to drop placing ads completely and simply use audience development combined with PR. And you know what? These artists and organizations are actually increasing their audiences and saving their budgets at the same time!

So in this day and age when people are wanting to get back to relating to each other, and considering the tough economic times, I would choose to transfer a little bit of money and a little time and effort towards an audience development plan. Audience development can accomplish the same results as marketing, it costs less, is more cost effective in the long run, and will build relationships with people who can become major supporters of your art/organization. Of course, the very best choice would be to use both marketing and audience development side by side and to remember that audience development is equally valuable, if not more so in my humble opinion.

EXTRA OR NECESSARY?

I wanted to take one extra moment to seal the deal of why I feel audience development is necessary and not just an extra to marketing. I was speaking to a colleague of mine recently, and we were discussing the fact that most organizations say that they do not have the funding for audience development programs, let alone funding for hiring a consultant such as myself. It made me realize that maybe most of the arts organizations in the United States are not committing to developing their audience. Maybe we are committing to marketing, but not to audience development.

Most organizations I know of are in need of a bigger and more inclusive (diverse) audience. I am seeing empty seats. Due to most existing audience demographics, in the future, there will be more empty seats. Is marketing alone doing the job then? This to me proves that audience development is necessary.

Let's explore a little bit more. When is the last time you asked a friend or family member for a recommendation for a doctor in your area? Did you set up an appointment? Most of us do. I know I did. One recommendation, free advertisement, did a better job than the 9 advertisements that could have cost $4,500 or more. Talk about a price difference in obtaining a new patron!

Sometimes you can get lucky with a particular ad and a new person will respond. However, are you more likely to keep the patron via this new ad or the patron via the word of mouth? It is more likely that the new repeat patron will be due to the word of mouth and not the ad (unless you have the time to follow up which is a great technique of audience development). Now what do you think would happen if you shifted the budget and put the $4,500, or part of this budget, into audience development programs to help create a buzz for you?

Marketing definitely has its place and can be very effective, but in this day and age of increased competition to get recognized, going back to good old fashioned relationship building or reasonably priced audience development programs, is worth a shift in budget.

The only reason some people may still shy away from audience development is the fact that it does take time and effort. It may not cost as much money, but building relationships does mean time with people and efforts placed on audience relations programs. I ask you then, if you want to build a quality audience, isn't putting in the time and effort worth it?

A SHORT HISTORY OF AUDIENCES OR THIS OUGHTA CHANGE YOUR MIND...

A few years back I attended a session at the National Performing Arts Conference (NPAC) that really had my inner geek cheering. Lynne Conner presented her research about the history of audiences. It was called *In and Out of the Dark, A Theory about Audience Behavior from Sophocles to Spoken Word*[3]. The good news is that she wrote a chapter with this title for *Engaging Art, The Next Great Transformation of America's Cultural Life*[4]. So even if you missed this lecture, you can read the chapter.

Let me give you a quick breakdown about the audience cycle. This breakdown is from my personal notes:

Audiences through the centuries:

Pre 19th Century – Audiences Ruled

- Audience was involved!
- Patron supported, audience engagement, professional audience reviews
- Pre-performances to explain ahead of time were common
- The audiences ruled the performance – could shout to do something over again or tell the artist how good or bad it was during the performance

19th Century – Artist Ruled/Audience in the Dark

- Invention of the light bulb
- Audience in the dark with the artists in the spotlights on the stage
- Separation of artist and audience – the curtain we need to get past
- Shhh...quiet!
- Funding from government now instead of audience members

20th Century – Organizations Ruled

- Public and charity support – nonprofit arts popped up
- Benchmark arts were the main attraction
- Booms in art productions and companies
- Audience becomes even more distant – but we had a hand in creating this
- Supported through taxes, grants and tickets/donations

21st Century – Audiences want to rule again, or at least be our partners

- Audiences want to be engaged and participate again!
- Less funding via government/grants so we need to build relationships with audience
- More individual artist companies again
- Social media marketing and fundraising is born! Your audience is helping you to succeed.

Audiences Ruled ------> Artist Ruled/Audience in the Dark -----> Organizations Ruled ------> Audiences want to rule or partner again!

We need to continue to build relationships and opportunities for our audience to participate and come full circle with co-authoring the arts. If we want cultural participation, we need to make the opportunities accessible. This is why audience development is important!

Okay, so now you understand audience development, what it is, what it is not, who it is for, and why it is important to get started today. If you are sold and have accessed my enthusiasm for audience development, press on! What is the first step?

THE HOW OF
AUDIENCE DEVELOPMENT OR
THE NITTY-GRITTY

KNOW WHO YOU ARE & BRAND YOURSELF

I have been putting it out there that in order to meet the people that we will click with, we need to know ourselves better first. Here is a quick homework assignment to help you to do this. Take time out to brainstorm words to describe who you are. Are you quirky, fun, contemplative, serious, helpful, caring? A dancer, singer, visual artist? What kind of dancer, singer, visual artist are you? After you generate your list of words to describe who you are, think about who your friends are. They must admire those traits that you have if they are your friends, and in order to admire, they must possess some of these traits too. In a similar fashion, your list of who you are will speak volumes about who your audience is and will be.

Also, make a list of traits that you admire in others, but may lack yourself. This list will help you with diversification for your team of support. Whatever you admire in others and you feel is lacking in yourself, these are the traits you can look for when considering who to build relationships with. For example, if you are a carefree artist, perhaps lacking in formal organizational skills, forming a relationship with someone who admires your spirit but is an organized person would be beneficial.

This list can also help you in terms of diversifying your audience in ways that make sense for you, not what everyone else thinks is diversification. Diversify from your heart and from the definition of who you are, not because it would be good for a grant. Your being you will get you a better grant, the right grant. Your being you will get you a better audience, the right audience.

I once spent half day working with a client, a past gallery owner in Denver, on her brand. She decided to switch gears completely in her life, but during this time, we had a great time brainstorming for the right name and image and the exact look and feel for her gallery. We started out asking some fairly basic questions in order to get to this fun part.

Here are a few questions to ask before making decisions about your logo, tagline, marketing (or audience development) materials, website, etc.:

1. **Who is your target audience? Who would you like to see enjoying your art? Is there a group that is not showing up yet that you feel would be a good fit?**
2. **What is your mission and how do you currently do business? What changes do you need to make?**
3. **Who is your competition and what sets you apart from your competition? Having and defining a niche is important.**
4. **What colors come to mind when you think about your art form and organization?**
5. **What are your primary goals for the year? What will your arts business look like five years from now?**

You can get a little more detailed. I happen to have my list of 20 questions I ask my clients, and there are books specifically on the topic of how to brand, but after answering these basic questions, you will get more of an idea what your brand is going to be.

We ended up changing the name of her business to fit her niche since it went beyond the basic gallery. She also had a jewelry shop and a boutique section of her store. Her Gallery became a Galleria. Plus, she happens to be Italian, so this fit very well with her specific image. The colors, basics for the logo, tagline and a beginning to the look and feel were falling into place easily due to sitting down and answering these few simple questions.

As long as you keep who you are in mind, your audience (both existing and potential), and your goals and mission for this year and beyond, a brand will start to form. After you have a brand in place, communicating with your audience will be much easier since they will be able to understand who you are the minute they see and read about you. Good branding is good audience development!

INDUSTRY STANDARDS VS. UNIQUE BRANDING

I wanted to take a brief moment to chat about branding and industry standards. I would like to use the classical music world as my prime example. I was doing some research on the branding of orchestras around the world. What I found was eye opening. Out of 50 plus orchestras, I only found 8 (maybe 10) that had very unique brands. This means that if you were to black out the orchestra name, you would have no idea which orchestra in the world it was. I happen to know that there is an industry standard for branding an orchestra so people and the community can identify with it easily, however, this type of branding is bland, lacks creativity, and actually could turn off potential audience members into automatically thinking that the orchestra is not for them.

One of the 8 orchestras that had a different brand was the L.A. Philharmonic. Their brand is tied into their conductor as well as their venue. This differentiates themselves from everyone else out there, and if you were to see a picture of the conductor and a logo, you would know which orchestra it is. The brand is fresh in design and the pictures of the conductor and orchestra are captivating, action oriented photos. This brand is exciting, and new people will be attracted to trying out an orchestra concert since it is not the typical branding. The brand matches who they are and what type of audience they would like to have. This means that their branding is in line with their existing and potential audience members.

To me, sure there are standards for depicting arts organizations and artists, but this does not mean that your branding has to be same old same old. There is room to be creative within industry standards so you can stay true to the industry as well as stay true to what makes your organization unique.

DECISIONS, DECISIONS...BROADEN, DEEPEN, AND DIVERSIFY

You have figured out your brand, and you realize you need to build relationships. Who do you need to build relationships with? The three words afore mentioned can save the day: Broaden, Diversify, and Deepen. I will share that these three words were lovingly learned from the Rand Corporation's *"The Rand Framework," A New Framework for Building Participation in the Arts* [5]. These three words changed my life, and they can change yours too! Let's review our definition of audience development:

Audience Development is the building of relationships with your existing (Broaden) and potential audiences (Diversify), through the use of specific audience relations programs (the how), in order for them to become more involved with your organization and/or art form (Deepen).

Broaden = More of the same

Diversify = New audiences

Deepen = Audience Involvement: subscribe, volunteer, donate, advocate

Each have their Yes's, Maybe's (Potentials), or No's

I recommend not bothering with the No's, but invest your time and energy on the Yes's and Maybe's. Every once in a while you can reassess the No's.

"Your audience gives you everything you need. They tell you. There is no director who can direct you like an audience."

~ Fanny Brice

BROADENING (GOOD FOR THE AUDIENCE, BAD FOR THE WAISTLINE)

KNOW YOUR AUDIENCES

Broadening your audiences begins with assessing your existing audiences. If you do not know the following about your audiences, I would survey and perhaps use focus groups to get to know them. The following is a list of organizational and sample survey questions:

- How many subscribers or members do you have?
- How many donors?
- How many volunteers?
- What are their common demographics: age, incomes, education level
- How many have children? What are their ages? Do they bring them to concerts?
- What do they like to do in their spare time?
- What other forms of cultural art performances do they like to attend?
- What other community events do they attend like sports, lectures, festivals, etc.?
- Do they like your venue? What improvements are needed to make it a more comfortable experience for them?
- Ask them about sample program formats and have them rank them on a scale of 1 - 5 on whether they would attend.
- Ask about your ticket prices and whether the price would effect their decision to go to these performances. What would they pay?
- How do they find fun things to do in your area? Which newspapers, radio, online, emails, etc.?
- Did they see or hear your ads in _____?

- How would they describe your organization?
- Do they like your artistic director?
- Do they like the staff?
- What improvements need to be made?
- Why do they attend?
- What do they like and dislike about living in your area?
- What performance would they like to see in the future?
- What is their favorite composer, playwright, choreographer, dancer, artist?
- What is their birthday (month/date only)?
- Do they donate to your organization? If not, would they consider in the future?
- Would they consider volunteering? Special events, community outreach, box office, ushering, in office, etc.?

I think you get the idea of what types of questions would be good for getting to know your patrons, and I bet you probably can think of other questions you are just dying to ask them! The key is to form a little bio about the audience member, who they are, why they live in your area, and why they attend your performances. You will then get a feel for their experience with your organization and with other parts of the community. With this information, you can find more people similar to them by:

- Developing artistic and educational programs that suit them
- Redesigning your brand and marketing keeping in mind the various demographics* and the psychographics** that resonate with them

---

Demographics research - the research on the characteristics of people that include age, income, education, occupation, household size, home ownership and home value, among other factors.

** *Psychographics research - the research on people's lifestyles and behaviors, including their interests and values.*

- Placing targeted ads in the right places
- Collaborating with groups that they would enjoy
- Making improvements that they will notice, which will create positive buzz
- Creating social opportunities for them

Further, you will now know what your organization means to them. Knowing why they attend and how the experience makes them feel can translate into a better mission or branding for your organization. Why they like the area and what they do in their spare time, these answers can can give you wonderful ideas for your future programs and events. Listening to your audience can give you the best advice for running your organization.

How often should you survey or use focus groups? I would say every few years is good since people and situations change. If you are considering making a major change, I would use your audience as a sounding board with surveys and focus groups as well. You don't want to inundate them with surveys or requests for feedback, but once in a while, when appropriate to do so is the way to go.

Since you now know your existing audience, you can begin to plan and implement audience relations programs that make sense to find more patrons that are similar to your existing audience. We will discuss audience relations programs soon.

Aside from surveys, I recommend getting to know people and supplying impeccable customer service to build relationships (more subjects we will be exploring soon). If you find out something interesting about someone, make a note of it to continue building their bios. The more you know, the better relationships you can build, and the stronger their relationship will be to your organization. This stronger relationship will lead to many wonderful things, including deepening their experience!

AREA AND ARTS RESEARCH

Besides getting to know your existing audiences, it is good to find out more about the area you are in. This is where you will find out all about your community! I like to use our government census bureau as well as local county and city demographic reports.

The statistics from these reports will tell you the demographics for your immediate population. You may find out, for example, their median age, how many people have an income between $50,000 and $100,000, what nationality is the most prominent in your area (we have a big Irish and German population where I am), and numbers on your Hispanic, disabled, veteran and underserved populations (etc). These numbers can be quite helpful in figuring out if a goal or program you have in mind would be valued in your community and if you have the numbers to validate implementing these ideas.

I also recommend looking at any arts related statistics if and when they are available. I happen to be a natural geek and seek out these types of reports. Learning that 23% of the population in Colorado goes to see arts events can be helpful, and finding out what percentage from this goes to events for dance, visual arts, museums, classical music, etc. can also be helpful. You may find out that people from a certain arts area do attend another arts area, etc., etc. The information in all of these reports is valuable to your audience development planning. I have included some helpful links in the Resources area at the back of this book to help you get your research started.

A BRIEF NOTE ABOUT DATABASES

Databases do need to be considered for handling the information that you find out about your audiences. There are books about how to find and maintain a database, but I wanted to make a quick recommendation. When it comes to databases, the more a database can handle all of your patron information and allow you the ease of segmenting your entire lists into targeted efforts via all the various demographics and psychographics, the better off you will be. For example, there are databases out there they can now handle all the ticketing as well as the development side of a non-profit business. Some of them even have scheduling modules that will allow you to keep track of all your audience development/marketing efforts, your grant writing, and your donor efforts. A few have specific modules for memberships, subscriptions, volunteer management, event planning, and class scheduling.

I would sit down and make a list of all the reasons you need a database and specifically look for one that can accommodate as much as possible in one database. Non-profits (and individual artists) are usually short staffed with not enough time to get everything done. Having a database that can help you in most of the facets of your business as well as give you the ability to have all your patron information in one place is definitely the way to go.

DEEPENING THE BONDS BY TAKING STOCK!

In the past I heard "deepening" described as moving your patrons down a patron pipeline, but I would rather move them up an enthusiastic ladder. To me, deepening refers to creating an experience for your existing audience that is so wonderful that they end up being enthusiastic enough to become subscribers, members, donors, sponsors and volunteers.

Deepening is furthering the personal touch. You want to give them the experience of a lifetime so they will come back again and again, and in time, offer support for you and your organization. You want your art/organization to mean something to them. You want your mission to speak to them personally. Use your audience surveys and feedback from your focus groups to evaluate and implement improvements that will deepen your audiences' experience.

You can also implement audience engagement or participation programs to deepen their experience, before, during and after an event to make them feel part of the process. I have found that when artists and organizations add these types of programs into their year and then ask "what was your favorite event of the year," most of the time, the audience chooses the events that had more built in engagement or participation.

After you have created a sensational experience, use all of the information from your surveys, focus groups, relationship building, etc., to ask the right people to:

- **Donate**
- **Volunteer**
- **Sponsor**
- **Become a Board Member**
- **Participate on a Committee**
- **Take part in a specific focus group in the future**

Deepening also can mean deepening your relationships with your audience members. Get to know them as individuals and find out about their personalities, their strengths and weaknesses, their talents, and their comfort levels regarding getting more involved. Again, it's akin to building a community for yourself and your organization. Your community will be there for you in good times and bad times, and their talents will become your talents, their strengths will become your strengths. Together you will be able to rise above the weaknesses by addressing their concerns and making any necessary improvements.

There are many ways you can deepen your relationships with your audience and deepen their involvement. Again, we will be talking more about these types of audience relations programs later.

In the meantime, let us take a look at the audience's experience cycle since it can help you to deepen your audience's experiences in a positive way.

THE EXPERIENCE CYCLE

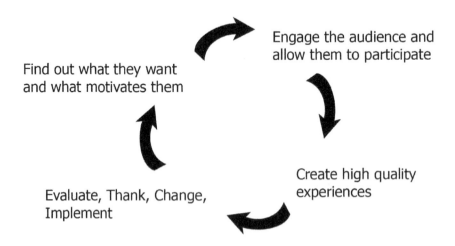

1. Find out what they want and what motivates them

This is where surveys and focus groups can be helpful. Asking the preferences of a few audience members that you know will give you some useful answers. These answers will help you with your programming, collaborations, venue choices, and customer service.

2. Engage the audience and allow them to participate

Since the audience wants to be part of the experience again, now is the perfect opportunity to create audience relations programs that engage the audience more and allow them to be a part of the event.

This does not mean that the audience needs to play a role during the event, although some artists and arts organizations are creating clever ways to do this, but as long as the audience feels a part of the process for the creation of art, they will feel engaged.

3. Create high quality experiences

If you really want the audience to keep purchasing and coming back, you need to create high quality art. Art that is not of high quality may have its place, but for obtaining people's hard earned time and money, "quality first" should be a big rule for you.

4. Evaluate, Thank, Change, Implement

This step is what I like to call follow-up and follow through. After the event or purchase transaction, you will want to connect back to the audience and get their feedback. You can thank them at this time and ask for their comments and suggestions. You will then want to consider making changes that are doable and make sense based off of their comments and suggestions. Lastly, you want to follow through by implementing these changes and letting your audience know that you cared enough to do this for them. Your audience will feel cared for, one of the 4 C's of audience development. This care will get them thinking positively about their experience with you and will allow the cycle to begin again. They will come back due to your caring nature and your thoughtfulness.

IN ORDER TO CREATE EVEN MORE CARE, I SUGGEST DELIVERING B.D.A.

What in the world is B.D.A.? Why it is **B**efore, **D**uring, and **A**fter of course! You want to treat your audience well so they know you care about them. This will in turn deepen your relationship with them.

Here is how B.D.A. Works:

Before – Impeccable Customer Care:

Give them the correct information, listen to their needs, and give them the best services and products, all with enthusiasm.

During – An Amazing Experience:

Provide high quality care, high quality art, a complete experience, audience participation opportunities, all with enthusiasm.

After – Fast and Friendly Follow-up:

Offer your thank yous in a timely manner, get feedback, implement changes for needs and concerns, make time to get to know your audiences, provide invitations to future events, all with enthusiasm.

If you deliver B.D.A. incredibly well, you will fall on the good side of the 3-10 people rule. What is the 3-10 people rule you ask?

3-10 PEOPLE RULE

Whenever a person has an incredibly bad experience or an incredibly good experience, people tend to tell 3-10 people about it. Making sure you give your audience an amazing, positive experience before, during and after can help ensure that people will tell 3-10 other people about this positive experience. It is word of mouth in the bag!

1,2,3...ENGAGE!

Engaging your audience and allowing them to participate will help you to build relationships with them and increase their interests for supporting you. Engaging also deepens their experience with you and your art. The audience relations programs you create will certainly help you to engage your audience and get to know them better, but just for fun, here is a list of some interesting ideas you can incorporate. Engage! - Get your audience to become more a part of your art experience:

Audience engagement and participation ideas:

- Talk during the event– behind the scene stories about the art, music, etc.
- Produce high quality every time you connect with your audiences
- Caring elements – when you take care of audience needs – tell them what you did
- Branding – let some of your audience members participate in the process
- Reminders – send out personal reminders to events
- Social Media – engage in conversations with your audiences

- Outreach and connect online using tools that engage them further
- Have an audience favorites event based on their votes/feedback
- Collaborating with other artists to give audience a bigger arts experience
- Giveaways and contests
- Signing CD's, Books, Posters, Artwork after the event
- Joking with your audiences – good natured fun
- Sometimes ask for comments during event and comment back
- Talk Withs after the event (Termed "Talk Back," but like "talk with" as a better term.)
- Invite a community group or organization to speak before/after if their mission closely ties in with your art programming
- For musicians, allow your audience to choose song from a menu (write-up a menu of songs for evening, but let audience choose what they want to hear next)
- Social Media comments and likes on your audience members pages
- Have them participate in surveys and focus groups
- Encourage that they send emails with feedback to you
- Ask them to volunteer at the event: information/merchandise tables, will call, etc.
- Ask them to close their eyes or open their eyes wider or breathe – help them take in your art in a more focused manner
- Ask them to sign a guest book or provide a doodle book to doodle in
- Have a reception after the event with artists, staff, etc. present for your audience to speak with
- Host house parties for smaller, intimate events
- Ask them to help with social media, website, and other online outreach projects
- Your original idea here!

Be sure that with whatever idea or program you decide to implement, it is something that makes sense for you and your brand, and will be comfortable for your audience. If you are not sure, ask your staff and audience for their opinion before implementing.

You have learned about how to deepen your audience's experience, which will help to deepen your relationships with them. Now it is time to discuss how to get your audience more involved with your art and your organization, the main goal of deepening your audience.

There are many ways to get your audience more involved. I have already mentioned the main ways. They can become frequent buyers by subscribing. They can become members. They can also help you with their time by volunteering. Of course they can support you by donating money or becoming sponsors of your art. Whichever way is best suited for them, there are ways to increase the likelihood of them getting more involved. Let us go through these different ways one by one, and I'll relate some best practices for you to use.

SUBSCRIPTIONS/MEMBERSHIPS

Some of you may think that subscriptions and membership programs no longer work. The reason they are no longer working is the fact that we are no longer putting in the effort it takes to make them work. I have seen current organizations and artists that put in the time and effort, and their programs are doing quite well!

What are they doing to be successful? I could do another entire book on this topic, which some authors have already done. Instead of reinventing the wheel, let's quickly go through the top best practices of using audience development for more successful subscription/membership programs. If you want to read more about this subject, I recommend reading Danny Newman's *Subscribe Now!* (details in resource section).

1. Do your audience development homework and figure out who is a potential subscriber or member from your existing audience. Are there people that are coming back piecemeal time and again?
2. Find out what your audiences really want by talking with your audience members.
3. Create packages and benefits with your audiences in mind. Do not create packages based on what you *think* they would want, but rather on what you *know* they want.
4. What audience relations programs would work for you and your audiences?
5. Treat your subscribers and members with first-class treatment.
6. Get to know them as people.
7. Provide them with opportunities to get to know each other too.
8. Remember you need to make this a priority in your time and budget if you want success.
9. It will take more time and effort, but it will be more cost effective for you in the long run.
10. Thank You, Thank You! - Be sure you have a solid thank you program in place for your subscribers and members.

As you will see in this handy chart [6] (exact monetary details may have slightly changed), subscriptions make sense and cents:

Marketing costs for	
Subscription Renewals	$.06 per dollar
Subscription Sales to previous attendees	$.27 per dollar
New Subscriber who never attended	$4.12 per dollar
Point of Entry Costs	$.50-$.60 per dollar
Single ticket sales to members of the family	$.35-$.50 per dollar
New subscriptions to members of the family	$.15 or less per dollar

Some Ideas for subscription benefits:

- Early purchase dates or special showings
- Discounts on future purchases
- Discounts for restaurants
- Discounts for other arts related events and purchases
- Special invitations to receptions, galas, etc.
- Discounts (or free) for workshops and educational opportunities – hands on events
- Special commemorative gifts and other forms of showing appreciation
- Discounts for friends and family (2 for 1 is an option)
- Special events with artists and directors
- Chance to be in a show, painting, etc.
- Package deals (restaurants, hotels, resorts, stores)
- Discounts on products they would be interested in
- Special attention – send birthday cards, random thank yous, up-to-date info
- Members/Subscribers Only section of website
- Badges or ribbons so they can proudly show they are subscribers/members if they wish

Remember that these benefits need to be what your audiences actually want, and not what you think they will want. You of course need to get to know your audience to find out what they actually want and need!

VOLUNTEERS - AUDIENCE DEVELOPMENT BRINGS OUT THE BEST IN VOLUNTEERS

Some people may want to offer their time to help support you. It is important to have a solid volunteer program in order to offer them this opportunity.

I have worked on many events and have helped to fill in as the volunteer coordinator. In order to put the word out in various places for the volunteer opportunities, I usually post:

1. In local papers
2. On Volunteer Connections Websites
3. Twitter
4. LinkedIn
5. Facebook
6. By sending out emails
7. By spreading the word in person

Can you guess where I had the most success? I found the majority of volunteers through using Facebook and emails. The people on the email list and on Facebook were the people that were more connected to the artists and the artistic director of the events. The people that want to volunteer the most are the ones that are connected and care about your art/organization already.

You can obtain volunteers from the outside sources, but they may not want to remain a volunteer for the long haul unless you start using audience development (relationship building) to get to know them. Part of audience development is learning about your supporters. For new volunteers, you will want to ask them basic questions to learn more about their preferences and reasons for volunteering:

1. What are their strengths and skills?
2. Do they like working with people?
3. What do they enjoy doing?
4. What job would they rather not do?
5. Why are they volunteering?
6. What ways do they want to be contacted?

7. What days and times can they volunteer?
8. What types of jobs have they had in the past?

I could go on with a few other questions, but I hope you are starting to get the picture here. Audience development makes volunteering all about the volunteer, not just about what the organization wants and needs. If you were to place a volunteer in the wrong position, you will lose the volunteer. If you do not relate to them in ways that are best for them, you will lose them. If you do not find out why they are volunteering, you will lose a priceless opportunity to figure out their reasons and possibly their goals for helping you. You might find out that they are volunteering because of a friend, or they are also an artist, or that they want to give back and they chose your organization since it speaks to them.

Getting to know the volunteer and placing them in the right position will make them more comfortable. Building relationships with your volunteers will also help uncover the passion behind the volunteering. Once a relationship is built, they are more likely to be put in the category of friends and family. Audience development will bring out the best in your volunteers and get them excited about volunteering again.

Overall, finding volunteers can be a great deal easier if you ask the people that care. Once you find the people that care and want to volunteer, get to know them as people (not just as your worker for the day). You will most likely find out that they are special in many ways and that their qualities will be just what you are looking for!

Your volunteer checklist:

1. Do your volunteer program homework
    a. Create job descriptions
    b. Format a volunteer profile form
    c. Get the word out about your volunteer opportunities

    d. Collect volunteer profiles

    e. Interview and place correctly

    f. Train properly – Orientation Meetings

    g. Staff is informed and informing

    h. Follow-up with your volunteers/staff, Evaluate, Make changes

2. Use Marketing & Audience Development to continue to find great volunteers
3. Find out what motivates them
4. Build a fun incentive program
5. Get feedback and testimonials
6. Think about Volunteer Memberships
7. Thank You, Thank You, Thank You! - Implement a Thank You Volunteers program

I wanted to note that in a few cases, people would volunteer to obtain the benefits from incentive programs I had set up. Incentive programs are a fantastic way to reward your volunteers for their time and efforts. Here are a few suggestions for benefits in an incentive program. Again, make sure that the benefits you choose for your program is what your volunteers actually want.

Benefits for incentive programs (based on hours volunteered):

- A certain amount of tickets
- A subscription/membership
- An invitation to special events, workshops, etc.
- A free gift of their choice (works great if you have branded items you sell)
- Volunteer bucks for purchasing music, art, etc.
- A special coffee date, luncheon
- Early purchase ability
- Special discounts and coupons for themselves or others

I have been at organizations that say they need help via volunteers, but sometimes they are not sure what types of tasks they can delegate to a volunteer. The following is a list of suggestions you can keep handy.

Ideas for volunteer jobs:

- Office work and research work
- At the event
- For fundraising, telemarketing, subscriber/member drives
- For grassroots efforts – flyering, word of mouth, social networks
- Outreach community events - tabling
- Ambassador programs
- Stage crews
- Email address collectors
- Special events
- Special needs – graphic/web design, grant writing, IT support
- Internship opportunities (you may be able to find volunteers that are interested)
- Committees and Board Members

We ended with Board Members for a reason. To me, having someone support your organization by joining your board is the ultimate volunteer position. Let's take the time to discuss what a good board would look like.

ARE BOARDS ONLY FOR ORGANIZATIONS?

Boards are not just for non-profit organizations. Boards are required for nonprofit organizations, but an individual artist or for profit organization can have a board for all the same reasons, to have a core group of people help you to build a strategic business plan, connect you further to your community, and help raise the financial and volunteer support that you need. Individual artists and for profit organizations can also use specific experts to help them, such as a lawyer or marketing guru. Don't be afraid to ask for "board" support even if you are not a nonprofit. We all could use a core team of supporters, right?

In any case, you want to have a well rounded board with members from various backgrounds so that they can help you in ways that you need help. You want people that will want to commit to the stipulations of being on your board. You want people that are good to work with too.

BOARD OR BORED

After attending various lectures, workshops and other educational sessions about better boards, here is my top list of points to keep in mind.

Considerations for a better board:

1. Get the right people on your board!

You want to make certain the people on your board will work well together and are ready to contribute. You also need a variety of people that have the backgrounds specific to what you and/or your organization needs.

2. Make sure they know about their job - create a manual for your board members

I highly recommend creating a board manual that has descriptions of their job duties and meeting expectations. You would be amazed at how many boards I have discovered that do not realize that their main job priorities are fundraising, strategic planning, and acting as an ambassador for your organization. Be sure the terms of serving are stated clearly as well. You can add information about your business so you can also use this manual as a recruiting tool.

3. Ask for a commitment with a signed contract

Getting them to sign on the dotted line after they have read the manual is a good way to see who is ready to commit and who is not. This contract will show them that serving on their board is an obligation to be serious about.

4. Keep them in the know

Make sure you have good communication with your board so they are up-to-date with what needs to be done. Group email communications are wonderful for this task in between meetings. These emails are a good time to let them know how close they are to their goals, and to let them know who is doing what (a little peer pressure can help).

5. Keep them enthused and keep it fun!

Food is always a good way to entice your board, but the way you conduct meetings and emails with them should be good natured too. Board members are people that are volunteering their time and energy for you. You want to make their volunteering experience special.

6. Introduce them to the staff

There have been times I have found boards that do not know the staff of their organization. Introducing them to the staff is the first step for good board/staff relations. It always good to put a face to a name and get to know people as, well, people.

7. Get them advocating for you out in the community – represent!

This is part of their job, being an ambassador for your organization. It is an important part of their job, so I am mentioning it again. There have been times I have seen board members that do not function as ambassadors or advocates for the organization. It is good for your board members to be people that attend functions and events on your organization's behalf.

8. Form committees and find people you can move to a future board

If you are a smaller organization (or individual artist), you can at least set up two very important committees – an audience development/marketing committee and a fundraising committee. Your committees are more hands-on members that help you to accomplish your goals. Committees are a great way of finding dedicated people that could be considered for a board position in the future.

9. Set up a cycle system so board members do not get burned out

This cycle is part of the terms of service. The best boards have term limits where the old and the new members overlap by one year. This way, there will be a year in each cycle where you have more people power for special task forces, projects, goals, and the old board members can help the new members acclimate.

10. "Thank You, Thank You!"

Be sure you have set up some program to thank your board members. These people have gone the extra mile for you, and you want to recognize and honor them for the work they have generously done for you. Award ceremonies and other formal events are never too over the top for appreciating this group of people. You can also get creative with your thank yous. Hopefully you will get to know your board members personally so you will be able to thank them in a way that is sure to be special for each person.

Another group of people that would be good to show appreciation for is your donors. I highly recommend setting up a donor program that takes all 4 C's of audience development into consideration. Connect with your donors; collaborate with them; build a donor community, and show your donors you care.

DONORS

Donors (and sponsors) need to be wooed now more than ever. Did you know that 80%* or so of your donations come mainly from individual donors? If this is not the case in your budget, well maybe it should be. In order to become better at soliciting donations, it is good to keep in mind the typical donation cycle:

---

* Various books and lectures give this figure.

Donation Cycle

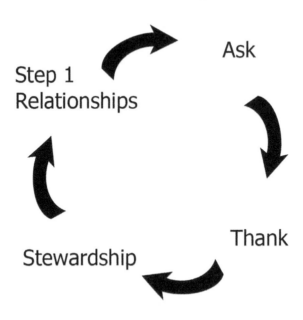

Step 1: Build relationships with people. Do not ask at this stage. Get to know people first.

Step 2: Once you are on friendly terms, then ask for their financial support. The ask will be easier since you know them, and they are more likely to give since they know you.

Step 3: Thank them! Have a thank you program in place.

Step 4: Continue building the relationship with your current donors and follow up with information about their donation.

Step 5/1: Start over with new potential donors.

In order to be successful, here are some suggestions to make your development process even better.

1. Do your audience development homework – find out who is in your area
2. Use the Six I's[7]

    a. Identify who your best donors would be by use of available databases

    b. Introduce & Interact – qualify your research by speaking with potential donors

    c. Interests & Needs - listen to them

    d. Inform - deepen understanding about the project/ organization

    e. Involve – acknowledge and engage their concerns and comments

    f. Invest – recognize and practice stewardship[**]

3. Get the right people on your team - Mavens, Connectors, Salespeople[8]

    a. Mavens are people that like to spread the word, these are the natural marketers of our world.

    b. Connectors enjoy introducing you to new people. These are the people that are always saying, "I want you to meet Jackie!" and start introducing you.

    c. Salespeople are the natural closers. These are the people that can seal the deal for raising funds or selling tickets or getting people to come to an event.

You need all three types of people on your teams.

[**] Stewardship is the follow up connection with your donors to let them know the results of their investment.

4. Find out what motivates donors – match with values

5. How does it benefit them and the community?

6. Suggest donation level

7. Create a benefits/recognition program - ask for comfort level

8. Get feedback and testimonials

9. Thank before you bank – have a thank you system in place

10. Stewardship – follow-up with your donors, keep in touch and tell them how their $ is working!

One of the best books on the market in teaching people how to build relationships for donations is *Relationshift, Revolutionary Fundraising* by Michael Bassoff (Steve Chandler, Robert D. Reed Publishers, 2001).

Some helpful facts and tips to consider[9]:

- It can take 6-10 interactions to obtain a new donor.
- 75-80% Individuals, 6% Corporate, 8% Bequests, 18% Foundations
- Corporations and Foundations have different motivators
- Corporations are allowed up to 10%, but rarely get to 1% (2-5% good)
- There is a delay in philanthropy during age shifts - these are the years of major changes Middle Age from 40 to 55, Older Age from 65 to 75, Adolescence from 18 to 28
- Learn how to listen and create profiles – use a database capable of creating the fields you need to accomplish this
- Make your donor messages memorable and unique
- Consider the setting for the ask
- Always talk to the couple and not individually
- Test out your ask first - prepare
- Be brief, memorable, to the point, with audience friendly presentations
- Many no's are really not yet's – discover and address concerns

- You can suggest more than one way to give
- Don't ignore the small donations – little gifts add up and you never know who is a millionaire in average clothing
- Have fun-draisers again! Add an element of fun back in!*

IDEAS FOR THANK YOU/APPRECIATION PROGRAMS

Your patrons and supporters would love to be thanked and appreciated from time to time. I usually suggest following the 3x thank you rule. This means that you will find at least 3 separate ways to thank someone for their contribution. A formal letter can be considered one way, but what other ways can you thank someone? Here is a quick list for you:

- Phone calls from Board Chair
- Phone calls from Board Members
- Handwritten thank you notes from Board
- Official letter for taxes – make memorable with a special note
- Special gifts and discounts
- Donor only information – special newsletters and reports (one page is best)
- Proper and timely Recognition Programs
- Special events with artists and directors
- Chance to be in a show, painting, etc.
- Package deals as a bonus (restaurants, hotels, resorts, stores)
- Special attention – send birthday cards, random thank yous, up-to-date info.
- Donors Only section of website with extra benefits
- Your great idea here!

---

* Don't Just Applaud, Send Money! by Alvin H. Reiss (Theatre Communications Group, Inc., 1995) is a good book about different kinds of fundraisers through the use of solid case studies.

DIVERSIFY FOR YOUR FUTURE!

"...building a consensus and understanding among people through personal interaction dialogue, and participation in the arts. It requires that you get in the trenches. A long-term process by nature, it also requires sensitivity, tenacity, persistence and courage."

- Donna Walker-Kuhne
Author of *Invitation to the Party*

To diversify means your organization reaches out to a different audience in your area that is not already attending or purchasing. After completing your statistics on your existing audience, you will know exactly who is not a part of your audience. Diversifying, in particular, has some extra homework involved for your overall audience development plan. You will need to know your area's demographics, the differences in how generations think, and what your area's psychographics are all about. As a reminder, psychographics are a way to gauge someone's personality. They may fit into the Baby Boomer demographic, but maybe they have a GenX mentality.

For starters, I suggest brainstorming what target audiences you would like to reach. Some popular examples are:

- Families
- Latino or other ethnic populations
- Generation X
- Generation Y
- Millennials
- Students and Faculty (if near a university)
- Corporate and Social Groups
- People who are attending a different art form

- People who are involved in civic activities
- People who volunteer and donate to other organizations

Once you form your brainstorm list, choose 1-3 of them to work on for starters. During your planning, you will want to consider what artistic programs you have chosen for the season. Is there an event that would be easy to target families? What about one that the Generation X crowd would enjoy?

With diversification it is extremely important to establish relationships before even attempting to market. The stronger the relationship and connection, the more likely that someone from the group will help you to spread the word. From all that I have read and experienced, marketing to a new audience will not work well unless you have established relationships ahead of time. You may see the occasional spike from a marketing effort, but in all honesty, there will be no lasting, continuing results.

Another note to consider, I would not try to reformat all your programming to be more palatable to a new audience. It will make all audiences feel like a bait and switch has occurred. Your existing audience will not be too happy and the new audience will be puzzled if the offering is a one time experience. Stick to what and who you are. The right audiences will appreciate you for being what and who you are. Of course if you were already considering experimenting with a new long term program that adds to your artistic quality, by all means use that artistic growth to your benefit and invite your new potential audience.

For example, if your season does not include factors that would appeal to children, yet you want to diversify your audience with family, you will need to consider your programming to reach this audience long term. If you find that who and what you are doesn't quite click with this potential audience, you may not want to make any changes and instead target a different potential audience that would be a better fit. However, if you find you are ready to grow in this direction, then plan on making your program choices more family friendly in general, or add a series of family friendly events and commit to this format long term. Simply offering a family event one time is not going to instantly bring you the family audience on a consistent basis. This approach applies to any outreach to a new audience.

Before we talk about the different forms of diversity, let's make sure we fully understand what diversity and other related terms mean. Here are some sample definitions from various sources:

Diversity - *the state or fact of being diverse; difference; unlikeness*

Inclusive - *including a great deal, or including everything concerned; comprehensive: an inclusive art form; not excluding any particular groups of people: an inclusive society*

Multiculturalism - *the preservation of different cultures or cultural identities within a unified society, as a state or nation; . the policy of maintaining a diversity of ethnic cultures within a community*

Source:

Dictionary.com, "Diversity" <http://dictionary.reference.com/browse/Diversity> (December 15, 2011).

Dictionary.com, "Inclusive" <http://dictionary.reference.com/browse/Inclusive> (December 15, 2011).

Dictionary.com, "Multiculturalism" <http://dictionary.reference.com/browse/Multiculturalism> (December 15, 2011).

Diversity statement:

The focus of this intervention is on recognizing the uniqueness in everyone, valuing the contribution that each can make because of those unique qualities and creating an inclusive work environment where awareness of, and respect for, those of different cultures is promoted. It is the quality of the work experience that is paramount.

Source:

Boulder Labs Diversity Council, "What is Diversity?" <http://www.boulder.doc.gov/diversity/diversity.html> (Dec. 15, 2011).

FORMS OF DIVERSITY

There are many forms of diversity aside from the typical race, age, gender and income that most of us cater to. Before going on to the next page, challenge yourself to come up with a list of different diversity categories.

Times up! Turn the page for my list...

Various forms of Diversity:

- Race
- Ethnicity - Ancestry
- Gender
- Age
- Sexual Orientation
- Special needs – physical disabilities
- Geographic location
- Income – economic status
- Religion
- Education
- Housing - Own vs. Rent and House vs. Condo/Apartment
- Marital Status - single, married, divorced
- Family
- Military status – active, veteran
- Employment - status, occupation
- Immigrant status
- Hobbies – passions
- Daily choices - newspaper, radio, television, restaurants, pets, type of pet
- Genetic make-up – hair color, eye color, height, medical background
- Favorites – food, music, artist, type of art, social cause
- Travel – well traveled, locations, etc.

There are books that dive into the uniqueness of each form of diversity. I have listed a few in the resources section at the end of this book. For now though, I recommend getting to know your new potential audiences by researching and building relationships with people within your community.

MARKETING VS. AUDIENCE DEVELOPMENT FOR DIVERSITY

So how do we begin to diversify? Do we simply use marketing toward another group of people? I am a firm believer that in the case of diversifying, simply translating your marketing is not going to cut the mustard. Here is where the differences lie:

Marketing for diversity is similar to:

The take a pill option – This is the quick fix solution. It is expensive, gives temporary results, and is glitzy and glib (programming, language, generalizations).

Audience Development for diversity is similar to:

The exercising a good lifestyle option– This is a long-term solution where you do the research, make the connections, build the relationships, make the collaborations, care about acknowledging each other's differences, and find what you have in common. This is more work since you will be meeting with people and finding out what their preferences are, then using your new found education in discovering and creating programs that they would enjoy. You will continue to follow up and build relationships to get these new audience members more involved. Despite the time and effort, this option works and is not as costly.

Before you attempt to diversify, you want to ask yourself the top 10 tough questions.

TOP 10 TOUGH QUESTIONS

1. Why do we want or need to diversify?
2. Have you ever felt like a minority?

3. What can you do to create more diversity in your own life?
4. What do we all have in common?
5. What types of collaborations do you think will have a good impact?
6. Have you ever created a program to be a point of entry?
7. Are programming changes really necessary?
8. Can education and audience relations programs bridge the gaps?
9. Are you ready to re-educate yourself about the world around you?
10. Do we really need to treat people differently?

If you still want to diversify after answering these questions, here are my top 10 suggestions for preparing yourself for diversity.

TOP 10 SUGGESTIONS

1. Go out and become a minority by placing yourself at places and events where you are the minority
2. Broaden your life with more diverse activities
3. Get to know owners of family owned restaurants and businesses
4. Make connections with organizations that already serve your potential audiences
5. Make connections and collaborations with other organizations
6. Learn their language
7. Brand for optimum diversity and consider all your audiences during this process
8. Become a part of your community by executing community outreach programs and by giving back to your community
9. Cater to all of your audiences long term when considering programming

10. Remember that we all want to celebrate, connect, and be moved

SOME DOS AND DON'TS TO DIVERSIFYING

The problem with many of the current suggested solutions such as special programming, hiring a more diverse staff, creating a more diverse board, and employing artists of various backgrounds, is that they may lack follow through with the new audience. For instance, you may recruit someone to be on your staff or board that is of color or of a younger generation or from a particular geographic location, but are you having this person reach out and build relationships or are you hoping the mere fact of having a "token" member on your staff (yes, I went there) will work wonders? If the latter, then people will see right through your "tokenism."

Hiring artists of various backgrounds as well as scheduling special programming can help to begin your efforts. Notice how I mention this will "begin your efforts." There needs to be follow up and follow through to build relationships so your new found audience will keep coming back and know that your attempts are not a one-time event.

From what I see, if you are not willing to put in the time and effort that is needed for true audience development, your diversity efforts will continue to have touch and go results. Let's get real! If you are not even remotely thinking that such and such art is for you, would one special art event get you hooked? Can you blame them if they don't come back with a one-time effort? The organizations and artists that are creating more diverse audiences have been doing the work that relationship building requires.

It also needs to be mentioned that if you are simply attempting diversity for the grant dollars, you have lost the meaning and the beauty of diversity. We need to stop treating our audiences as numbers and start treating them as people.

Without further ado, I present you with a random list of dos and don'ts in terms of diversifying your audience:

- Do your homework and find out if your potential audience would enjoy your art.
- Do format a three to five year plan in which you reach out and build relationships with new groups of people.
- Do stick with the plan over the years and tweak as necessary.
- Do create programming that is enticing for your potential audience.
- Don't expect them to understand your art right away. Don't expect them not to understand your art right away.
- Do educate about your art if necessary.
- Don't create one-time programming and expect this will do the trick.
- Do follow up with your new audience and start a conversation with them.
- Do continue to build relationships through more programs of interest.
- Do set up a task force or committee to help outreach to your potential audience.
- Do diversify your own life by building relationships with people of various backgrounds, attending new and different events, etc.
- Do learn what it is like to be different.
- Do learn their language.
- Don't expect "token" recruits to diversify your audience.
- Don't expect them to come to you. You may have to go to them.

- Do understand that people of a different background may need to learn to trust you as people before investing their money in your art.
- Don't simply translate your marketing and expect this to return big results. It's not the language that brings them in, it is how you understand them as people that will start the relationship.
- Do realize that they may purchase differently or have different preferences than what you have in place. If you have done your relationship building, you will know what you need to implement to make them more comfortable.
- Do find opportunities to collaborate with a variety of organizations and groups.
- Do personally invite people that may be interested in helping you build relationships with their communities.
- Do keep the conversation going.
- Do learn to brand your marketing so all diverse groups involved will appreciate you.

With well thought out audience development planning and a good helping of time and effort, you can build a more diverse audience. Do understand that despite our differences, we can all enjoy high quality art!

No matter if you want to broaden, deepen, diversify, or a combination of the three, you will need to be able to build relationships with people. If the thought of getting to know people makes you nervous, and you need some advice, let me attempt to make you feel a little more comfortable.

BUILDING RELATIONSHIPS – IT'S EASIER THAN YOU THINK!

Richard Wiseman, PhD, is a professor at the University of Hertfordshire in England. Wiseman's title is Professorship in the Public Understanding of Psychology. I found out about him and some of his ideas through Oprah.com[10]. He offers the following points to ponder when it comes to meeting people (the first step in building relationships):

1. *Your mindset sets the stage for meeting the right people.*
2. *A typical person knows about 300 people on a first-name basis.*
3. *Meet someone new and you're "only two handshakes away from 300 times 300 people;" that's 90,000 people.*
4. *By the same logic, if you meet 50 new people at a conference, you're just a couple of introductions away from 4.5 million opportunities to change your life.*

If you are still feeling a little nervous about meeting new people, I found the perfect book for you. *Face to Face: How to Reclaim the Personal Touch in a Digital World,* by Susan RoAne. RoAne has also acknowledged the fact that our digital world can make it challenging to meet people face to face, and we have lost practice. After reading this worthwhile book, I have formed my list of top 10 suggestions.

My Top Ten Suggestions from *Face to Face: How to Reclaim the Personal Touch in a Digital World* by Susan RoAne[11]

1. Start with small talk – learn to be knowledgeable about current events and a variety of topics and use a visual hook (weather, compliment, observation).

2. Use relevant responses, stay on topic, and ask intelligent questions.
3. Join groups – get out and network – community outreach.
4. Act like a host even if you are not the official host – make them feel comfortable.
5. Think about what you have in common.
6. Become a matchmaker and always give credit and refer people.
7. Turn off your cell phone and really listen!
8. On the phone, make sure it is a good time and if they are pressed for time, cut to the chase or schedule a better time.
9. Stay in touch even if you need nothing - "HAY" calls (How are you?).
10. Be a good friend and treat people like you want to be treated.

By now I hope you are feeling a little better about learning how to meet people in the real world again. It will take a little practice. When it comes to audience development though, meeting people is essential. After meeting people, the nitty gritty of audience development begins, your efforts in building relationships. This is where designing a good plan comes in handy, but you will need to do a few "before the plan" tasks first.

BEFORE THE PLAN

YOUR HOMEWORK ASSIGNMENTS

I have spoken to many people behind arts organizations that do not know where to begin when it comes to audience development. All they know is that they need to increase their audiences and to build a better audience in general. Many of them have taken shots in the dark to attempt to figure out what programs work and what programs do not work for them, but they have yet to discover what to do to take some of the guess work out of their efforts.

I recently met with a marketing committee of a local organization that wishes to pursue audience development for this year's goal. The email immediately focused on programs that may work. What I encouraged them to do first was their homework. Just when you thought school was over, the school of life gives you an assignment.

Audience Development homework is the gathering of the facts, visions, and goals before the planning of programs can start. It is imperative that this homework be done to create the most thoughtful programs to suit your individual and organizational needs. The following is a quick list of homework assignments to get you started:

1. Figure out the demographics in your area so you can know what types of people are living in your community. You wouldn't want to plan a program for a particular demographic only to find that it is a low percentage of the population. The best way to find these statistics is to visit the US Census Bureau website and your local county website.
   http://censtats.census.gov/

2. Pull data and past surveys about your existing audience and format a generalization about them. It may also be a good idea to form focus groups to get personalized feedback. If your surveys do not give you details about your audiences' lifestyles, you may want to conduct a new survey with questions that will help you get to know them better.

3. After you have the details, you can create a character story about a general audience member to give this type of personality a name and background to refer to in all your audience development and marketing efforts. This will help you in terms of knowing what type of person to build relationships with and how this type of personality functions in their day to day life – their behaviors, their likes and dislikes, their beliefs, their general lifestyle. Get as detail oriented as you can.

From this characterization of your most common audience attendee, you will not only be able to find ways to attract similar patrons, but also ways to connect further with your existing audience base.

Here's an example of a character story:

Mary is 54 years old, married, and enjoys attending local community arts events. She and her husband are subscribers to the Philharmonic as well as patrons of the Art Walk Tour every year. Her only daughter moved out of state. Mary has two grandchildren and loves to spoil them when they are in town. She volunteers as a community outreach advocate for the Humane Society and is active at her church. Mary works part time at the YMCA and has her own consultant business on the side. She enjoys reading, going to lectures, hiking, biking, and spending time with her friends and family. Mary's choice for information is the Daily News and NPR and her favorite television show is Dancing with the Stars.

What we can infer from this characterization: Mary is a baby boomer, empty nester, who enjoys the arts (a variety) and is involved in her community. She attends functions with her husband, but may opt to go out with other friends and family. She spends quality time with her daughter and grandchildren when they are in town for the holidays. Her religion/spirituality is important to her. Her health is important as well and opportunities to learn are welcome. She has her own income and has an adventurous, entrepreneurial spirit.

Of course the best way to form a profile is to get to know each of your main attendees extremely well so a real characterization can be formed.

4. Figure out what target groups you would like to build relationships with to diversify your audience. Use your demographics to find out if it is possible. Research the groups' cultures, their belief systems, their lifestyles. Pinpoint the common ground and the organizations and groups in the area. Begin to develop a long term relationship with the group starting with a conversation to open an ongoing dialogue.

5. Learn how to ask and ask often. The best examples of audience development in terms of deepening involvement with an organization are churches. Churches, in actively performing their missions, ask their attendees to donate and volunteer during almost every contact they have with their audience. They post in bulletins, on the website, during the sermon, after the sermon, in their newsletters, at smaller group functions, etc! Most arts organizations are shy about asking due to increased competition and the feeling that they may be burning out their supporters. The key is to continue to ask new people and not just the already committed patrons. However, if a church needs to finance a new addition to their building, do you think they wouldn't ask the already committed supporters? They would ask everyone!

The main lesson we can learn from churches is that they are really good at audience development. Someone important will know your name and life story in no time at all and get you involved on a committee. It is daily clockwork for them.

6. Sit down and consider your goals, desired outcomes, and your program visions for an audience development plan. Who do you want to see in your audience? What would increased participation look like? What programs do you think would reach your target audiences? What will your volunteer program look like after your efforts? What are your fundraising goals and what programs will help you to reach those goals. Having a common visual of your desired outcomes will keep the entire team on the same page and more motivated with this extra homework effort. Every meaningful outcome begins with a dream or visualized desire. Get it in writing! A draft of your visualization to keep as a reference is extremely helpful.

By doing your homework and educating yourself on who your existing audience is, who to reach out to in your community, how to reach out, and what your desired outcomes and goals are, you are setting the stage for the beginnings of a well thought out audience development plan. Your future audience will be broad, happy and loyal.

PEOPLE POWER PLANS – YOUR CONNECTIONS!

Your next homework assignment is to draft your people power plan. Remember how each of us knows at least 300 people by name. The challenge is to come up with as many as 100 people that would be able to support you in the ways that you specifically need help.

Use an Excel spreadsheet format. You will need to document:

a. Person's Name

b. Contact Information – Phone, Email, Address

c. How they can help – Volunteer, Donate, Collaborate, Sponsor, Market, etc.

d. Maven, Connector, Salesperson (remember from *The Tipping Point* by Malcom Gladwell)

Your People Power Plan:

Name	Email	Phone	Task	M/C/S
Joan	Her email	Her phone #	Send out emails	M
Bobby	His email	His phone #	Hand out postcards	M
Sue	Her email	Her phone #	Talk to Rotary Club	S
Katy	Her email	Her phone #	Intro to Alumni Assoc.	C
Bill	His email	His phone #	Volunteer at concert	M

M=Maven, C=Connector, S=Salesperson

Again, try to come up with 100 names by starting with people that you know well to fairly well. Think of people that may know other people that could help. Start connecting and asking people if they would want to help!

- People you know, such as family, friends, colleagues, want you to succeed.
- You never know until you ask!

AUDIENCE RELATIONS PROGRAMS

Can be used to Broaden - Deepen – Diversify

An audience relations program is any type of program that will help you to build relationships with people. They can be a typical marketing platform that is tweaked to add elements of follow up so you can get to know your audience members. These programs can be used to Broaden, Deepen or Diversify. As long as you have an element of relationship building in your programs, your programs can be considered audience relations programs. Here are a few examples:

- **Word of Mouth (Buzz) Campaigns** – Make these programs more personal with personal invitations, education, and follow up networking
- **Grassroots Campaigns** - You can create attention grabbers in the community that will bring the audience back to you. Be sure to add an element that will get them to call you or visit you.
- **Business Card Campaign** – Hand out cards with meaningful messages that will get them to take action to contact you
- **Social Media** – Build a team of people and start connecting and engaging with your audiences
- **Subscriptions/Memberships** – To deepen your audience, create meaningful benefits your audience will actual want
- **Social Gatherings and Parties** – Can be thank you's, pre-concert, after concert events – build a team of social butterflies that will interact with your audiences and take note of what you find out
- **Group Sales** – Get to know groups personally and implement benefits they would enjoy
- **Corporate Relations** – Get to know people in the corporate world, get them engaged and ask them to become a partner in getting employees more involved

- **Donor Relations** – Get to know your donors and get them more involved
- **Thank You Programs/Appreciation Programs** – Audiences want to feel appreciated so create programs that make them feel thanked in more than one way
- **Impeccable Customer Service** – Create a B.D.A. Program
- **Ambassador Programs** – Form a team to represent you to spread the word, ask for support, etc.
- **Referral Programs** – Your patrons can help refer, make sure you have incentives that make them happy too
- **House Parties/Meetups** – Engage with smaller groups
- **Coffee Talks** – Plan on having coffee with specific people to build relationships and collaborations
- **At the Event - Talk With- Panel Discussions** – Provide your audiences with opportunities for education and participation
- **Personalized E-mail Campaigns** – Personal, one-by-one, no mass emails here
- **People Power Plans** – Your top support people – segment for other audience relations program
- **Surveys** – What does your audience want, what are they thinking?
- **Focus Groups** – Good for pre-planning, segmenting audience to get to know them better
- **Community Outreach** – Join your community and use opportunities to outreach
- **Collaboration/Partnerships** - With organizations in the community, create mutual benefits
- **Programming** - Tie in with community organization, cause, event, a theme that is important to your audiences
- **Partnerships with sponsors** – Build relationships with your sponsors so they help promote

- **Education programs** - Workshops, seminars – educate your audiences
- **Online Tools** - Blogs, discussion boards, online surveys, online networks - engage in 2-way communication!
- **Text Messaging** – Create a team that will send out personal messages to spread the word
- **Branding/Target** - From name of programs to design, be sure to get audience feedback to find out what they would identify with
- **Testimonials** – Stories – let your audiences tell their stories
- **Improvement Implementation** – With audience feedback, make improvements and let them know what you have accomplished for them
- **Publicity Campaigns** – Get to know your media people
- **Personalized Form Letters** – Write notes and personalize each letter – segment letters if there is more than one level of patron on your list
- **Newsletters** – Attempt to personalize – find a way that goes above and beyond the name field
- **Your Own Program Here** – You are a creative person, right? You can create a program that will get you more connected with your audiences!

No matter what program you choose to implement, you will want to keep in mind during the development stage that the main goal is to build your relationships by using a personal touch. You will also want to keep in mind to add an element of enthusiasm for your programs. Without enthusiasm, a well intentioned program will fall flat since your audience will feel your lackluster performance.

THE PLAN, THE PLAN

You will want a section of your plan for each objective that you have (Broaden, Deepen, Diversify). First title your plan The Audience Development Plan of _____. Your first section will be to define your current audiences. Then you will have a section for each objective you choose to do for the year and make sure you state the reasons why you are choosing to do this objective. For example's sake, let's choose that we would like to Broaden our audience.

A QUICK EXAMPLE OF A PLAN

2011-2012 Audience Development Plan for Orchestra X

Current Audience

Our current audience base consists of people with the following demographics, psychographics and other attributes:

Demographics:

Psychographics:

Attributes:

Objective 1: Broadening our Audience

In order for Orchestra X to serve a bigger percentage of our community, we choose to broaden our audience base. After pulling the statistics of our area, our goal to broaden this base is possible. There are _____% of people that fit our demographics, etc. Broadening makes sense, etc.

Specific Goal 1: Broadening our Boomers

Reason for this specific goal stated here.

In our area there is a _____% of Boomers. From the Arts Report X, _____% of the population in our state has reported it enjoys going to see an orchestra. Right now we have _____% of this demographic in attendance. We feel that we have not reached our potential for serving this segment of the population, nor have we tapped into all of the population that would enjoy seeing an orchestra, based on our research.

The next task is to select the audience relations program for each of your specific goals for broadening and then take the time to define each of these programs in your plan. The logic model is often used to define a program. I like to use a short form version of the logic model in order to get your plan done more quickly and efficiently. Here is an example of what each program in your plan would look like:

Audience Relations Program 1 (This format is a simplified version of the RAND Corporation's *Logic Model*)

Description – Name of program and describe how the program would work in detail

Cost: Include staff time, materials, consultant time, venue, etc. - budget

Who: Staff, Volunteers, Board, Committee, Partner? What will each person do?

Outcomes: Intended change in knowledge, skills, attitude or behavior

Indicators: Specific measurable numbers for the outcomes

Data Source: Who has the information and how will they provide it?

Evaluation: Data? Survey? Focus Group? Interview? Work?

When creating a program make sure it is unique to your own art form and organization. You want it to stand out and be memorable!

Putting this all together – a quick sketch example of a plan:

2011-2012 Audience Development Plan for Celebration Brass Quintet

Celebration Brass Quintet current audience Statistics Here

Objective 1: Broaden Volunteers and Audience

Reasons here and area statistics.

Specific Goal 1: Broadening brass quintet fans by using volunteers

Reasons and area and report statistics

Audience Relations Program 1:

Brass is Class – An Ambassador program using audience volunteers and other brass players to send out emails/social media messages with links to listen to sample files. 2For1 coupon code in message for them to redeem - each ambassador has a special code which will be input at online box office to keep track. Audience members will need to input the friend's email as well. Ambassador with the most redeemed wins a prize. Need 3 redeemed to qualify.

Cost: Cost of setting up mp3 files if any

Who: Shoshana announces via email and sets up codes for each ambassador, inputs in box office; one volunteer to organize, keep track of the program, at least 10 ambassadors to carry out message by email, social media, online groups

Outcomes: Increase in numbers

Indicators: Gain of 25 - 50 audience members

Data Source: Box office numbers from box office and number of coupons redeemed

Evaluation: Feedback from ambassadors and from people they spoke to via email, survey, or in person, amount of coupons redeemed

Collaborators: Fellow classical music organizations to ask for ambassadors

Thank you/Follow up: Email to thank and ask for feedback, ambassadors invited to thank you party after the event!

You can use a worksheet to help you draft each program for your plan. Here is an example of what your worksheet can look like.

YOUR AUDIENCE RELATIONS PROGRAM WORKSHEET

Choose: __Broaden ____ Deepen____Diversify

Program Choice (off list provided):_____

Character Story:

Your People Power Plan:

Name	Email	Phone	Task	M/C/S

M=Maven, C=Connector, S=Salesperson

Relations Program: _____

Description:

Cost:

Who:

Outcomes:

Indicators:

Data Source:

Evaluation:

Collaborator(s):

Thank you/Follow up:

At the end of your plan, add a section for a complete evaluation at the end of the year. Make sure you have:

- What are your current audience numbers now?
- Feedback about your audience relations programs
- General overview of whether your plan worked or not
- Ideas of making your plan better the next time around
- Or, if goals were accomplished or have changed, thoughts about future goals

After evaluation, you will have a better grasp on what worked and what did not work. Audience development is an ongoing process, and evaluating your efforts is a sure way to keep on a positive path to success.

WHY ALL THE FUSS ABOUT NUMBERS?

I realize that some of you may be thinking, if audience development is all about building relationships, why is the plan so laden with numbers? Audience development's main goal is to get to know your audiences. The other goal is to increase your audiences and supporter bases. We can use numbers to evaluate if we are indeed doing this. Usually when you focus on the relationships and form good partnerships with your audiences, the numbers you seek will naturally occur, but planning for these numbers is a good process to further ensure success. You will need to know the numbers for where you are starting and the numbers for what you would like to achieve. Again, these numbers will serve as an evaluation basis to let you know whether your relationship building, your audience relations programs, are working or not. Always remember though that these numbers represent real people. The ultimate goal of any audience development plan is to have happy and loyal patrons that support you, and for you to support them in return.

LAST MINUTE ADVICE FOR YOUR AUDIENCE DEVELOPMENT PLANS

In order for an audience development plan to work, 4 elements need to be a part of your plan. If you do not have these elements, the plan will not work. You need to:

1. Have all 4 C's in your plan somewhere. Your Connections need to be a part via your people power planning. You need to Collaborate with people and create win-win programs. You need to learn how to be a part of your Community and to build your own personal community of support. Lastly, you need to show people that you Care about them. You need your audience to know that you care as well as showing that you care for your supporters. Without all these elements in your plan, the plan will fall short.

2. Have a team to implement the plan. Having your marketing staff be the only people that contribute to making the plan happen will have your plan fall flat. A team mentality is crucial. You need as many people to help implement as possible. Each individual person has their own circle of people they are connected with, that they can connect you with. The more people that implement properly, the better the team. The better the team, the more likely you will have a very successful result.

3. Get the plan in writing. I know many artists that would rather skip this step, but having a neat and organized written plan

will allow you to manage your time and resources better. Also, getting it in writing is a commitment to audience development.

4. Remember the 5th C's to carry the plan out: be Courageous to step up and implement your plan, use Consistency to follow through, and have the Conviction to make the time and effort to get the job done.

When you have all four legs of your plan in place, you won't falter or wobble, and your plan will have the support to be successful.

A BRIEF BRIEFING...

I was having coffee with one of my colleagues, Amy Calhoun, and I realized that there is a section that I was leaving out. I would like to address the pitfalls for each discipline. I have noticed that each discipline has their own set of challenges. These observations are generalizations, so I recommend reading through the entire set. Call me crazy, but sometimes generalizations are very true to life. For example, there is an old joke that you can guess what a musician's instrument is by how they dress and carry themselves. I know people that can guess within two instruments, and usually one of them is correct. We, as humans, tend to be a little predictable at times since we align ourselves with similar behavior to others that are similar to us. Our bad habits can also brand us. The following set is the bad branded behavior that is typical among each discipline. When it comes to audience development, think about whether you fall into these generalizations and attempt to replace this behavior with more positive behaviors so you can more effectively build your audience.

VISUAL ARTS

I have many visual artist friends and have been to many open artist studios and arts festivals. I have noticed over the years that lack of follow through is the main audience development downfall that visual artists have. For example, I was at an arts festival and I happened to be admiring a photograph. It happened to be in the wrong size for me, and I asked if she had this print in the size I was looking for. She said it wasn't with her, but she had that size at home. I gave her a business card, and I never heard from her again. Another example, I had bought art from two artists at the Open Studios art event last year. Neither artist followed up with me to see how I was enjoying my art.

Perhaps visual artists are more into their art than playing host to their patrons. However, in times when it is so important for standing out from the crowd, finding your best patrons, and selling your art work, it is crucial to follow up with people. If you want people to be loyal to you, you need to be loyal to them first!

DANCE

I feel dance companies are getting better at following up with their patrons and incorporating audience engagement programs. For the dance world, it would be best to let people get to know your dancers as people! A biography in the program is not enough. I happen to be a big So You Think You Can Dance fan, a show which has brought new life and interest to dance in general. One key aspect of this program that works well is the fact that we get to know who these dancers are and become loyal to the dancers we enjoy the most. It is not uncommon for patrons to want to go to performances specifically because a certain dancer was cast. So, why not play up to this fact and allow your audience to get to know the company dancers as well. In order to create loyalty, the audience needs to feel connected with your dancers, and if you develop more opportunities for the audience to become acquainted with them, you will create a loyal audience base of support.

THEATRE

The theatre world has been the best at discussing the audience development issues in general. I have enjoyed many conversations surrounding the issues and challenges for theatre audience development. However, I feel there is a need to push past all the discussion of the issues and to actually focus on the solutions, and how to implement these solutions. There is nothing wrong with the discussion mode except when you get stuck there. There is a smaller percentage that is pushing past this, but it would be great to see the industry as a whole take part in promoting solutions and carrying themselves into the next phase of audience development, more implementation of the solutions. In theatre's defense, there is a small percentage of innovative folks that are blazing trails by experimenting with new styles, platforms, and play productions. Theatre as a whole can learn from these entrepreneurs of their discipline.

CLASSICAL MUSIC

In the realm of classical music, which happens to be my main background, there is also the problem of getting stuck in all the discussions. I have seen the same discussions resurrected decade after decade. It is time to push past this, but while this is a big problem, this is not classical music's main downfall. Classical music companies also need to follow up more with their patrons so they don't continue to slip through the cracks. However, even this point is not their main audience development problem.

The main problem: there is still that big elephant named Elitism trumpeting around the room. Classical musicians in general need to start connecting with their audiences and present their music in ways that take themselves down from the pedestals they have put themselves on. Gone are the days that we can rely on placing an advertisement and expect the audience to come to us. Instead, I suggest beginning to reach out by connecting with our communities again and meeting our audiences where they want to be, and start presenting in ways that they can connect with us, the musicians, and perhaps invite them to be a part of the planning process. There is a revolution slowly starting, and I hope this new trend will continue. The chamber music and solo musicians are paving the way. The new technology, especially for the bigger opera and orchestra companies, is also a positive step.

The more we can connect with our audiences, the more we can build relationships that will create many positive returns.

FILM

I recently read an article about the movie "The Help" in which they were wondering if black audiences would take to this movie. Since the movie was told in the voicing of a white woman, the answer was a big "No." Although later I found out that this audience did attend, due to some very talented actors that were a must see. A film, how it is produced, who is telling the story, who is cast for the part, seems to have some predictability as to who the audience will end up being. The trick is to find ways to relate to a more diverse base of people. In terms of audience development for film, diversity is the biggest issue. How to break past the general public perception for your movie and allow it to appeal to other groups of people – this is the big challenge for building your audience. The best advice I have for the film industry is to pay attention to the types of movies that do go beyond a smaller demographic base. Which movies do you see everyone in your area enjoying? Which films, when you go to the movie, have the most diverse audiences? Of course not every movie will appeal to everyone, and maybe for artistic reasons you do not want to cater beyond your vision, but if you want a bigger audience, maybe you need to broaden your horizons a bit too.

INDIE ARTISTS

The Indie Artists are a creative bunch, but their main challenge is relying on others to get an audience to notice them and become loyal to them. Indie Artists would rather spend their time creating, but when the product is themselves and their music or art, Indie Artists need to be extremely involved in their own audience development. I happen to see that the groups and individuals that do spend time getting to know their audiences themselves and are building relationships among their communities are the ones that are becoming more successful. The good news is that technology and social media is making it possible to easily start doing some of your own audience development and marketing. It is time for you to get in touch with your fans and more personally involved with them. This can increase the likelihood of becoming the next Indie Artist success story.

MUSEUMS

Museums are currently working on audience development. Museums have realized that they need to listen to their audiences more and find out what their audiences want out of their visits. They are finding out that their audiences want to be engaged. Many museums are incorporating audience participation programs via hands-on, interactive experiences. Some of these ideas are quite innovative. The important point to remember is that you want to not only engage your audience, but you want to connect them back to the art, which means you do not want to forget your core missions. Yes, you want your audiences to have fun in connection with the art or artists. Your challenge is to provide hands-on, interactive experiences that will educate and connect them to the art as well as be entertaining. You want them to get to know the art and artists more intimately through these new programs.

As I mentioned before, these are mainly generalizations. Your main issue may fall under a different discipline's, or you may be working through all five of these challenges. Whatever your main issue is, I recommend identifying it and then formatting solutions to overcome it and succeed.

ANOTHER BRIEF BRIEFING...(HOW MUCH TIME WILL THIS TAKE?)

My friend, and artist Annette Coleman, called me one morning, and we proceeded to discuss audience development and the arts, and what is making it challenging for some artists. She asked the question whether or not there was a formula I could give her and other artists. I replied that there really isn't a set formula for all artists since each artist is unique.

I so wish I could give you a magic formula, such as, if you spend this amount of time and ask this amount of people, you will see this amount of audience, etc. Life, unfortunately, doesn't fit into a nice and neat little box. We do attempt to make life fit into boxes, but it seems to me that the more we work outside of these mentally created boxes, the more we will be able to develop ourselves and our audiences.

What did come out of the conversation is the fact that audience development takes time and effort, and in the beginning, this time and effort will need to be spent discovering what will work best for you. This means that there will be trial and error time to find out what tools and resources work for you. You will need to evaluate the amount of time you need to spend on these efforts, how many emails to send, how many phone calls to make, which outreach efforts work, and what social media and marketing methods get results. The good news is that you will discover what you enjoy doing and what works and what doesn't work. If the two are at odds with each other, say you hate Twitter, but find it is working for you, this is the time to evaluate if you can ask someone else to help. If you enjoy Facebook, but it hasn't been working for you, perhaps you need help with tweaking the way you use Facebook to make it successful.

We also discussed how the methods of audience development may be difficult for people whose brains may not work in that fashion.

Annette suggested that spreading the word and the task of building relationships can be more of a left brain effort in some instances, and most artists tend to be more comfortable working with their right brain. This means that during your trial and error efforts, you do need to be honest with yourself about what you are capable of doing.

You also need to consider that at first audience development can bring you out of your comfort zone with some of the tasks, and it can also be uncomfortable asking for help. However, once you get past these uncomfortable zones, you will not only realize what you can and cannot do, what works and what doesn't work (so you can rid yourself of tasks that waste your time), but you will be able to build a team of people that complement your weaknesses with their strengths, to help you build your audiences.

Audience development methods do work when implemented properly. What works for you though, may not work for others, and you personally need to be comfortable with the programs and processes that you choose to do. Audience development is not a one-size-fits-all solution, but it can be a solution for you when you figure out how to tailor and size it specifically for you and your arts business.

SNEAK PEEK AT BOOK II
THE TAO OF AUDIENCE DEVELOPMENT

I have taken you through the basic fundamentals of audience development. You should now feel comfortable with starting to create your plan. If you get stuck, I am only a phone call away.

Now on to my philosophies about audience development. Book II, the Tao of Audience Development will be coming out soon. Tao (pronounced Dow and sometimes spelled Dao) is literally translated into "the path" or "the way." The Tao philosophy taps into living with more simplicity and harmony and being more natural and one with nature. I believe that audience development is a more natural way to build your audience.

I have hand picked some of my favorite blog posts over the course of five years. These entries will give you a feel for audience development in this new way. Instead of simply the nuts and bolts, as you have just experienced, you will be getting a big dose of my enthusiasm for audience development. I will share why I think it is super important to start sooner than later, some of my thoughts on the current state of affairs for the arts sector, and a few discussions about audience development in terms of arts advocacy and other current events in our world.

The following are a few samples. Happy Reading!

AUDIENCE DEVELOPMENT AND THE NAME GAME

May 25, 2010

<u>Name</u> (from dictionary.com): —noun

1. a word or a combination of words by which a person, place, or thing, a body or class, or any object of thought is designated, called, or known.

One of the first tasks of a parent is to name their newborn child. Parents usually put a great deal of consideration into naming their children. There are books and websites with a plethora of choices because names have meaning, names are an identification for a lifetime, so the choice is important. At times a name can be a cherished heirloom handed down from generation to generation, our namesakes are special to us. Our name, in one sense, is a brand for life. We can change our name legally, but most of us become attached to the name our parents give to us.

Well then, how does a name relate or translate to audience development? One of the 4 C's of audience development is "Caring." The quickest and easiest way to show you care about your patrons is to make sure you know their names – to remember their names, how to pronounce them and how to spell them correctly. Learning someone's name is the beginning of building a relationship, so it is important to get their name right.

I have often posted this audience development tip of the day: learn an audience member's name and make sure you spell and pronounce their name correctly. I thought it was time to finally expand upon this so there is no confusion as to why this seemingly common sense tip is a big deal. Let me give you a few examples.

When I was a box office manager (actually in many of my sales/customer service positions) I made it a point to get to know my customers and to learn their names. One day during a major subscription drive, we were dealing with close to 500 different patrons. One of our patrons preferred to come in to renew his subscription. I had met him after one of the concerts the year before. I greeted him with, "Hi Bob! Are you here to renew your subscription?" He looked at me in awe and exclaimed, "Wow! You remembered my name!" We went on to have a conversation about his programming tastes, and I helped him choose the best subscription for him. I also found out about his main hobby, which translated into a nice item for our silent auction later in the year. The success of this conversation, resulting in a subscription sale (an upgrade from his original plans) and his increased involvement via a silent auction donation, all occurred due to the fact that I remembered his name!

In terms of pronouncing and spelling names correctly, I will share another personal story. With so many communications bombarding us, seeing our name spelled incorrectly is an easy filter, telling us to not bother with a piece of information. My name, Shoshana, is often mispronounced and misspelled. Most of the time it can be quite amusing, but at times when people are approaching me to ask me to become more involved, or to donate, I am not amused. Most people aren't. If our name is misspelled, we zone in on it and feel a little slighted. If I see an ask letter from an organization that has misspelled my name, I tend to recycle those requests without opening. If someone continually mispronounces or gets my name wrong, I tend to not want to be supportive with their request. You see, if you do not care enough to get a name right, one of our biggest identifications in life, then it is showing that you do not care about the person. The person will not want to donate or become more involved if you are unable to accomplish the easy task of spelling their name correctly. Not spelling their name correctly will show that you only care about what you can get from the person. If you have name mistakes on your list, and they are not corrected, it is communicating that these people are only a number to you. Names matter due to our identification with our names.

Getting someone's name right is important in any form of communication. Misspelling a name in an email or even a Twitter DM will be noticed by the person. The person can communicate that you misspelled their name, but if you become savvy to the error, don't be shy, apologize for the error. It will show that you do care enough to notice and correct. Our names are important to us. Let's show others we care by getting their names right!

It may take some time and energy, but a great way to connect with your patrons is to simply pick up the phone or send a more personalized letter asking them for proper spellings. When you are meeting people, take the time to not only learn peoples' names, but how to properly pronounce them. Learning someone's name correctly can open the door to bigger and better opportunities. If you do not have a good memory for names, you can use little mnemonic tricks, such as associating something about their physical appearance with their name. Getting someone's name right shows that you care, and they will be more interested in you and your communications (your needs) in return.

So the next time you are doing a mailing or meeting people, play the name game. You will get extra bonus points for getting the name right!

AUDIENCE DEVELOPMENT FOR THE ARTS END OF YEAR A-MUSINGS

December 29-30, 2010

Today I have been thinking about the year 2010. With all the "Best in 2010" articles floating around, it can't be helped. At this moment though, I have been giving much thought to New Year's resolutions.

2010 is nearing the end and a bright and shiny 2011 is due any day now. What would you do differently next year? What new ideas and programs will you want to implement? In terms of audience development, here is my "best of" advice to my fellow artists and arts organizations:

1. Find your niche! I cannot stress this enough. With all the new artists and arts organizations popping up, it is extremely important to differentiate yourself from everyone else. If you have not discovered your niche, ask yourself the following questions. What do you do better than anyone else? What is your main focus? If others have similar missions, what makes you different from them? In a world of saturation, you need to define what makes you special. This defining will help get you in touch with others that relate to your niche.

2. Brand yourself correctly so the right audience can find you. After discovering your niche, make sure your brand matches and helps promote your niche. It is time to individualize your marketing. In my humble opinion, the reason why some artists and arts organizations get overlooked is due to the fact that their branding is just like everyone else's. I see the same old types of photographs, messages, missions and programs that everyone else is doing. No wonder people may think the arts are not new and exciting! It is time to be the artists that we

are, creative individuals that push beyond the status quo. Let yourself be brilliant, and brand yourself so there is no doubt as to who you really are.

3. Put the passion back into everything you do. It is such a buzz kill to hear artists belly aching about not being recognized, not being paid enough, not selling enough, not having enough gigs… Guess what? The audience can pick up on these vibes. We need to ask ourselves again – Why am I creating art in the first place? We need to put the passion back into creating and enjoying our art. A positive vibe will also be perceived by the audience and will translate into positive actions (more sales for one). Let's be completely honest. Maybe the arts are suffering due to lackluster offerings. Maybe we are lackluster since our passion has been replaced by righteousness or the "we deserve better" attitude. Art comes from the soul. Without passion, the soul cannot produce high quality art. With passion, the soul will be joyful and create offerings that other souls will be drawn to.

4. Don't be afraid to ask for support. All artists and arts organizations need support, but many of us are afraid to ask for it. Why? I had a discussion yesterday about this very point. I came to the conclusion that the reason we may have trouble asking is that we do not define our art in terms of a tangible product. Maybe this needs to change. The arts (proven time and time again) have many beneficial gifts for our society. They benefit the individual and our communities. This means that the arts can be defined in a tangible sense. The arts are worth supporting due to these benefits. Do yourself a favor and get over being too shy to ask for support. You have a

product that is worthy of support. Define all the benefits of your art and make it easy for someone to relate to the reasons why your art is worth investing in.

5. After you realize you and your art are worthy, ask in a personal manner. This is the other reason why people may not be supporting your art. You need to ask personally! We as individuals are inundated with donation requests. Sending a form letter is going to end up with all the other form letters, "filed" in the trash. The reason people give to one particular cause over another is that they feel connected to the cause. Connect with people again and ask them personally for support. If you know so and so, don't send them the same old form letter, write a personal ask to them or take them out for coffee. Form letters are not working anymore, and we have been hiding behind them due to our fears of asking for help. Get up the courage to relate personally again. You will find all the support you need this way.

6. Collaborate more! Due to the saturation point of the arts and the economy, we need to collaborate more, not less. We need to get over the mentality that "there is not enough to go around" and instead share in the bounty that is here. I want to challenge you to find at least one creative collaboration for 2011 and put your passion into it. Take the time to look around you and see how we can help support each other!

7. Discover the talent that is in your own back yard to expand your resources. I hear people talk about capacity issues, but there is an easy solution. I could get in trouble for discussing this one, but I feel that, when we are hiring new people, we are too hung up on the qualifications and letters after their names.

Of course, if you need to see a doctor you want a qualified one. However, the talents of individuals can go unnoticed and unused due to this mentality. For example, I was looking for a graphic design artist. I interviewed several for the job. There were some that had the fancier degrees and some that didn't. I actually ended up hiring a person that was intelligent and talented, someone without the fancier degree. You see, education is important, but so are the individual gifts, talents and experiences that we have. Do not overlook someone simply based on credentials. Do not place someone strictly based on credentials either. Instead, take the time to discover that person's individual gifts and how they can be useful.

8. Deliver impeccable customer service! I want to remind you that when we have an extremely positive experience or when we have an extremely negative experience, most of us will tell 3-10 people. Now that we have social media, these numbers are vastly larger. For example, yesterday I read someone else's blog about how poor the customer service was for a business he had to deal with. He sent this blog to his list of Twitter Followers (around 450) and he probably sent it to his Facebook friends as well. I bet he even sent out a few emails to his closest friends and family. Some of his followers, family, and friends probably forwarded to their circle of people. It would be fair to say that his bad experience with this company, his story, was told to at least 1,000 people. Yowza! Next, consider whose opinions we value the most – opinions from our friends and family. Double yikes!

In this age of blazing fast communication, it is extremely important to give your patrons the best service possible, before, during, and after your event. When the service is incredible, people will talk favorably about you and your art, and your wonderful story will spread across the land. With our world becoming smaller and smaller due to social media, "the land" is bound to be international (more to think about).

9. Fast and friendly follow up, please! I know I have <u>blogged about this topic before</u>, but it needs to be mentioned again. Many artists and organizations are not following up with their patrons. Part of the reason may a be lack of keeping good data so you can follow up. Another factor is the old "I simply don't have enough time" excuse. If you are scratching your head wondering why your patrons are not following up with more purchases, it is probably due to the fact that you are not following up with them. When you drop the ball, it sends a message to your patrons that you don't need their patronage again. Period.

I recently framed my Linus Maurer with the little message he sent to us. If Linus can take time out of his busy schedule, I'm sure you can too. Following up is more valuable than creating marketing for new purchasers, so allocate a little of your time for this important task. Keeping a relationship with your existing patrons will reap many benefits, and it costs less to follow up (versus obtaining a new patron).

Remember the old adage: Make new friends, but keep the old, one is silver and the other is gold. If you do not keep a good database that allows you to follow up, consider obtaining a better way to keep your records. This investment is completely worth it. After you have a good system in place, develop a program that creatively keeps you in touch with your patrons. Above all, any reason to thank them is a good reason to get in touch.

10. Implement changes when needed. The worn out excuse "that is how it has always been done" is simply, in a word, weak. With our world evolving at lightning speed, we as artists and arts organizations need to change too. Traditions are only traditions because we have made them so. Consider making new traditions. Here is a list of items to consider:

- Your Board (if you have one). Are the right people on your board? Are they doing their job of fundraising and strategic planning? Are they advocates for your organization – do they build relationships in the community on your behalf? If the answer is no to any of these questions – your board needs to change.

- Is there something your patrons complain about? Develop a solution and tell them about it – make the changes to make them happy!

- Is your marketing/brand bland and like everyone else's? Refer back to the beginning points in Part 1 and change!

- Are the people who are volunteering or being paid to support you actually supporting you? If not, make a change!

- Are you getting to know your patrons as people? If not, make a change and get to know them.

- Are you taking time out to connect with people? Coffee, lunch, dinner? If not, go out there, connect, and change.

- Are you thanking your patrons enough? If you are not thanking them at least 3 times per transaction/donation – make a change!

- Are you asking for support personally – again, refer to Part 1 and change.

- Is your business structure working for you? If not, make a change.

- Is your programming working for you? Ditto.
- Are you engaging with your patrons? No? Change and engage!
- Is your mission current? If not, make a change.
- Are you following up? No? Then change and begin to follow up.
- Do you have a good database for keeping notes about your patrons? No? Take some of your change and make this change!
- Are you collaborating and becoming a part of your community? No? Change!

I think you get the idea. Sometimes it takes action before your entire team can be motivated. Someone needs to make a change so your world, your circumstances, can change.

With 2010 coming to an end and 2011 beginning, take the time to breathe and to sort out what is working for you and what is not working for you. Look around at all the new solutions that have occurred during the year. Create solutions that are best for you and your patrons for a brighter new year.

One of the wisest men who ever graced our earth said:

"Be the change you want to see in the world." – Gandhi
What do you want to see?

APPENDIX A

"One person can make a difference and every person should try."
- John F. Kennedy

Arts Media Coverage Campaign for Audience Development

I believe as a society we need to reconsider the value of the arts for our community and for our humanity. The arts have been with us since the beginning of time. We express our culture and history through the arts. It educates us and is a part of what makes us human.

The arts also have a positive impact on our economy, even in bleak times. People want to escape and get an emotional charge in these tough times, and the arts supplies this need. When people attend an arts event, they also tend to go out to eat or get a social drink before or after the show. This $28 average per person (more or less depending on your area) that goes back into our local economies can add up. However, since the loss of arts coverage, people do not know about where to go and what to attend. Many local arts organizations have been in existence for 30-50 years and people still don't know they exist.

With each day passing, many arts organizations are struggling to stay alive, some have gone under, and coverage is becoming bare bones. Some may view the arts as a luxury, but I say that the arts are a necessity in our lives due to all the benefits.

If you support the arts and know the value of the arts for your life, your children, for our culture and our humanity, please consider writing to your local newspaper and television station to ask for more coverage for the arts. Not only will it help the

arts and our economy, but it will help the news become more balanced as well.

I live for the day that there are daily reviews of arts events, and I live for the day there is an artscast in every television news program. Sports have been the main focus. It's time the arts became a main focus too!

For more information, please visit: http://buildmyaudience.com/arts-advocacy/

ACKNOWLEDGEMENTS

I could not have made this book happen with out the help of the following people. This book is dedicated to all of them. Thank you to:

- Richard Quenon – for being my constant supporter throughout the entire process.
- My mom, Leah Danoff – for cheering me on and helping to edit.
- My sister, Ilana Rudnik (a.k.a. Literal Lucy) – also for being a great cheerleader and an amazing editor.
- Nancy Filice for her graphic design expertise
- Annette Coleman and Amy Calhoun - for the wonderful coffee conversations that sparked new material.
- A. Richard Turbiak – for being my constant audience development colleague in Boulder, CO.
- BCAA (Boulder County Arts Alliance) – for bringing me awareness about audience development in the first place, back in 2006.
- Rosh (Brain Rocheleau) and The Blind Cafe^{TM} - for being one of my very first clients and for allowing me to use the experience as an example.
- My Twitter Followers – who became a support system during the entire 3 years time.
- My other colleagues, friends and family members – for all their encouragement.

END NOTES

1   Wikipedia contributors, "Marketing," Wikipedia, The Free Encyclopedia, http://kiwix.org:4201/A/Marketing.html (accessed December 14, 2011).

2   Wikipedia contributors, "Relationship Marketing," *Wikipedia, The Free Encyclopedia,* http://en.wikipedia.org/w/index. php?title=Relationship_Marketing&oldid=176834176 (accessed December 14, 2011).

3   National Performing Arts Conference, Lynn Conner, "In and Out of the Dark, A Theory about Audience Behavior from Sophocles to Spoken Word," 12 June 2007.

4   Lynne Conner, "In and Out of the Dark, A Theory about Audience Behavior from Sophocles to Spoken Word", in Steven J. Tepper and Bill Ivey, eds., *Engaging Art The Next Great Transformation of America's Cultural Life* (Taylor & Francis Group, LLC, 2008).

5   Kevin F. McCarthy and Kimberly Hinnett, commissioned by The Wallace Foundation, *A New Framework for Building Participation in the Arts* (RAND, 2001).

6   Bradley G. Morison and Julie Gordon Dalgleish, *Waiting in the Wings: Larger Audience for the Arts and How to Develop It* (New York, New York, American Council for the Arts, 1987, 1993), 175-176.

7   Thomas D. Wilson and Association of Fundraising Professionals, *Winning Gifts: Make Your Donors Feel Like Winners* (John Wiley & Sons, 2008), 8-16.

8   Malcom Gladwell, *The Tipping Point, How Little Things Can Make a Big Difference* (Back Bay Books/Little, Brown and Company, 2000,2002).

9   Thomas D. Wilson and Association of Fundraising Professionals, *Winning Gifts: Make Your Donors Feel Like Winners* (John Wiley & Sons, 2008).

10 Ben Sherwood, "How to Get Lucky" *O, The Oprah Magazine,* From the February 2009 issue of *O, The Oprah Magazine* <http://www.oprah.com/relationships/ How-to-Get-Lucky/1> (December 15, 2011).

11 Susan RoAne, *Face to Face: How to Reclaim the Personal Touch in a Digital World* (A Fireside Book, Simon & Schuster, 2008).

BOOK BIBLIOGRAPHY

Bassoff, Michael and Chandler, Steve. *Relationshift: Revolutionary Fundraising.* San Francisco: Robert D. Reed Publishers, 2001.

Beaudine, Bob. *The Power of Who: You Already Know Everyone You Need to Know.* New York: Center Street, Hachette Book Group, 2009.

Borads, Juana. *Salsa, Soul, and Spirit, Leadership for a Multicultural Age.* San Francisco: Berrett-Koehler Publishers, 2007.

Gladwell, Malcom. *The Tipping Point: How Little Things Can Make a Big Difference.* United States of America: Back Bay Books/Little, Brown and Company, 2000,2002.

Johnson, Lisa. *Mind Your X's and Y's.* New York: Free Press, Simon & Schuster, 2006.

Korzenny, Felipe and Korzenny, Betty Ann. *Hispanic Marketing: A Cultural Perspective.* Burlington/Oxford via China: Elsevier, 2005.

Morison, Bradley G. and Dalgleish, Julie Gordon. *Waiting in the Wings: A Larger Audience For the Arts and How to Develop It.* New York: ACA Books, American Council for the Arts, 1987, 1993.

Newman, Danny. *Subscribe Now!* New York: Theatre Communications Group, Inc., 1977,1983.

Reiss, Alvin H. *Don't Just Applaud, Send Money!* New York: Theatre Communications Group, Inc., 1995.

RoAne, Susan. *Face to Face: How to Reclaim the Personal Touch in a Digital World.* New York: A Fireside Book, Simon & Schuster, 2008.

Tepper, Steven J. and Ivey, Bill, Ed. *Engaging Art: The Next Great Transformation of America's Cultural Life.*

New York: Routledge, Taylor & Francis Group, LLC, 2008.

Walker-Kuhne, Donna. *Invitation To The Party: Building Bridges to the Arts, Culture and Community.* New York: Theatre Communications Group, 2005.

Wilson, Marlene. *The Effective Management of Volunteer Programs.* Boulder: Johnson Publishing Company, 1976.

Wilson, Thomas D. and AFP. *Winning Gifts: Make Your Donors Feel Like Winners.* Hoboken: John Wiley & Sons, 2008.

All books are available at the ADS website: http://www.buildmyaudience.com

RESOURCES

ADS website: <u>www.buildmyaudience.com</u>

Books, grants, resources, blog posts, and other helpful information

Other resources are listed on the ADS website.

ABOUT THE AUTHOR

Shoshana Fanizza has been a natural marketer and audience builder since she was three. Her mother caught her rearranging the soup cans at the grocery store to create a better display, and during her passionate performance, she attracted her first audience! When she was six, Shoshana volunteered before her sister's band concert to help fold programs for the local High School Band Association and proudly exclaimed to her mother, "I made some friends, what did you do?" Since this time, Shoshana is hooked on building relationships to help others on their arts journeys.

Seriously though, Shoshana has been involved in the arts all her life (horn, piano, theatre [Thespian status], choir, voice and dance lessons, puppets, art and jazz history classes, film enthusiast) and has a background in marketing, sales, public relations, customer service, and working for and with non-profit organizations just shy of 20 years.

From 2005-2007, she was the Marketing and PR Director for the Boulder Philharmonic Orchestra. It was at this position that she began using audience development in addition to marketing. Shoshana was part of the Boulder County Arts Alliance's 2006 Audience Development Initiative, and this opened an entirely new way of building audiences for her. Shoshana switched to a focus of building relationships and sold out Macky Auditorium's 2,000+ seat house, and house totals were increased by an average of 25-30% per concert. She developed their volunteer incentive program, expanded the marketing and publicity program, and was a primary team member in their fundraising, special events, and corporate sponsorship program. Some of her other positions have included Sales Manager and Customer Service for Karnes Music, Founder and Arts Administrator of the Celebration Brass Quintet in Chicago and Marketing Director of the Chicago Brass Choir.

In 2008, Shoshana founded Audience Development Specialists and is their Chief Audience Builder. After attending several arts marketing conferences, seminars and workshops, it had come to her attention that several experts define audience development, but do not show how to implement. This is why she founded ADS and decided to roll up her sleeves to not only inspire others about a new way of building audiences, but to work with artists and arts organizations to design solution based audience development plans and projects that work! Shoshana has a vision to help the arts by creating and implementing solutions for audience building, and her mission is to help people build supportive audiences that are a right fit specifically for them.

Shoshana is an idea person, and her enthusiasm is contagious! Through workshops she inspires, and through her hands-on work with organizations, she builds audiences. In 2012, she authored the eBook *The How of Audience Development for the Arts: Learn the Basics, Create Your Plan*. A follow up eBook, *The Tao of Audience Development for the Arts* was published in 2014.

She has been blessed to work with a variety of talented and quality artists/organizations. After working with ADS, all of her clients have enjoyed more positive people energy surrounding their art. On average, Shoshana's audience development techniques have resulted in a growth rate of 30-50% for audience numbers and monetary support, and she has never left a workshop, meeting or phone session without at least one "great idea!"

Shoshana has presented audience development seminars and workshops for the Boulder County Arts Alliance, Portland Piano International, Pro Musica Colorado Chamber Orchestra, and the Tampa-Hillsborough County Public Library System. She has presented at the National Arts Marketing Project Conference from 2011-2013.

Shoshana desires to work with artists and arts organizations that are ready for the opportunities that audience development offers.

Contact Information
Shoshana Fanizza
Audience Development Specialists
720-722-4ADS (4237)
ads@buildmyaudience.com
http://www.buildmyaudience.com

"Never treat your audience as customers, always as partners."
~James Stewart